GET THE TRAINING VIDEOS THAT GO WITH THIS BOOK FOR FREE

To say thanks for downloading this book, I'd like to give you 29 WordPress training videos that go along with this book. Just click below to get your videos.

CLICK HERE TO GET YOUR VIDEOS

(Or go to gazellish.com/book)

D0035403

TABLE OF CONTENTS

Start Here (Book Extras)

Welcome to Step-by-Step WordPress for Beginners!

In this book, you're going to learn how to go from an idea all the way to a completed website that's live on the web for your friends, family, or customers to see.

Having a website of your own enables you to connect with others, build an audience, start or grow a business, stand out in job interviews and networking situations, and so much more.

But paying a web developer to build a website for you can be REALLY expensive, and learning to code can take forever.

That's where WordPress comes in.

WordPress makes building a website relatively easy, quick, and inexpensive.

All you have to do is learn the basics of how to use WordPress, and the possibilities are endless!

That's exactly what you'll learn in this book: How to build a beautiful website on your own domain from scratch, no matter how little you know about websites or WordPress.

There are two main sections to this book, but before we cover that, there are a few things to know before starting this book:

THIS BOOK COMES WITH 29 TRAINING VIDEOS

I actually used to sell these 29 videos as a course for WordPress beginners, but I'm giving it to you for free because you purchased this book.

To get the videos that go with this book, go to:

GAZELLISH.COM/BOOK

(That's my website, so don't worry, I'm not sending you to some strange site!)

Create a username and password, then create your account

You should be redirected directly to the video dashboard, and you're good to go!

Use those videos as a supplement to this book, or vice versa.

My #1 goal is to show you how to use WordPress to get a beautiful website up and running in no time without the confusion, so I'm hoping the videos help you do just that.

THIS BOOK ALSO COMES WITH A FREE WORDPRESS THEME I'VE CREATED FOR YOU

That's right, I've created a WordPress theme for you so you can get started learning and tinkering in WordPress without having to purchase a premium theme right off the bat if you don't want to.

I designed this theme specifically with the readers of this book in mind.

It's based off WordPress's default TwentySixteen theme, so you'll have to have the TwentySixteen theme installed in order to use it (which should come installed by default with WordPress).

I think you'll find I've made it to where it's easier to customize, and I've also added in a number of must-have features for entrepreneurs, bloggers, and businesspeople.

I think you'll like the look and feel of it a lot, and it's built with clean code straight from WordPress themselves so you know you'll be running a good theme on your first WordPress site!

To get your free website that goes along with this book:

GO TO GAZELLISH.COM/BOOK AND CREATE YOUR FREE ACCOUNT

Once you're registered and you're inside the video dashboard, look for a link in the navigation at the top that says "Tools".

On the Tools page, you'll see the link to download the theme file. Click that to download the theme I've made for you.

We'll get into how to install a premium WordPress theme in a later chapter, so for now just download the theme file and you're good to go.

Note: The child theme I created for this book is far from perfect, but I'll be making changes and fixing style issues as they arise. If you install it and notice any issues, email me at mike@gazellish.com or use your 1-on-1 WordPress Help section of Gazellish.com (after you're logged in).

WHAT WILL YOU GET OUT OF THIS BOOK?

As I said, this book and the accompanying videos are designed to help you go from absolutely nothing but an idea all the way to a beautiful, finished, live-on-the-Internet website.

So if you're a complete beginner - I'm talking "what's WordPress?" type of beginner - you're in the right place.

This book is divided into two sections:

The first section is a quick-start run through for complete beginners. It includes chapters 1-15, they're very short, and most chapters build on the one before.

The second section is more "intermediate" and includes task-specific things like SEO and theme customization. These are sections you'll want to have on-hand once your site is up-and-running and you have a better understanding of how everything works in WordPress.

What's even better is, nearly every chapter in both sections of the book has a video that goes along with the same topic.

All you have to do is login to your Gazellish.com account (register at gazellish.com/book) and they're waiting for you there.

Okay, so that's what you'll hopefully get out of this book, but here's a little about me, the author.

WHO AM I?

My name is Mike Taylor, and I'm a WordPress developer, marketer, and entrepreneur.

I realize those are REALLY broad titles, so I'll try to elaborate.

I originally started out in business and marketing. Among other things, I worked in retail, sales at an automotive service department, and business insurance for a large insurance company.

Years ago, while I was working in sales, I started learning to code with basic languages like HTML and CSS. After spending some time building basic websites on the side, I left my insurance sales job to work for a marketing agency.

It was the perfect mix: I got to work on websites and design, but also on the sales and marketing strategy. It was in that role that I learned about WordPress. I started teaching myself how to use it, and I learned just how powerful of a tool it can be for practically anyone to use.

Over the next couple of years, I spent every day working with small businesses and entrepreneurs, helping them build and market WordPress websites in order to drive traffic, leads, and ultimately grow their business.

After a couple of years at the marketing agency, I decided to start my own WordPress web development company. I then spent every day focusing on one thing: building WordPress websites that would make my clients' money.

While I was building WordPress sites for clients, I kept hearing the same thing:

"Can you make some kind of video or take screenshots showing me how to use my new WordPress site?"

See, I would build them a site in WordPress, then they would want to go in and add posts, pages, make edits, etc. After all, that's really the beauty of WordPress - being able to make changes yourself.

The problem was, WordPress isn't exactly "simple" for anyone unfamiliar with it.

So I started making videos for some of my clients, then one day decided I should just turn them into training videos that any beginner could use.

I put together the 29 videos you get access to with this book, and I wrote this book to accompany the videos.

Now the two work together, and hopefully you'll find a ton of value in the work I've put in here.

WHY DO YOU NEED TO KNOW ALL OF THIS?

The last thing I want to do is waste your time, so here's what you need to know about me:

I build WordPress websites professionally and have been doing so for several years

I've also spent a significant amount of time working as a professional marketer, so I know how to grow websites as well as build them.

Most importantly, I learned WordPress years ago by doing what you're doing right now, so I can relate to where you're at!

So whether you're starting from scratch or already have a foundation in WordPress, this book and the videos that go with it should help take your WordPress skills and website to the next level.

Now let's get started!

Note: Images in this book may appear blurry due to the resolution of the screenshots. The images still serve their purpose, but I pre-apologize for the resolution difference.

01: What is WordPress?

Before we can even think about building a website using WordPress, we first need to know what WordPress is.

For starters, <u>WordPress</u> is what's called a content management system (or CMS), and a CMS is basically a system used to manage the content of a website.

Without a CMS, website owners would have to either learn how to code or ask a developer to alter the source code of the pages of their website anytime they wanted to make changes.

CMSs like WordPress make it extremely easy to manage and edit a website with little to no coding knowledge.

But WordPress is more than just an easy way to manage a website. It provides the actual framework for a website, too.

Think of a website as a house. There's the foundation, frame, and walls, then there are the cosmetics that give each house its customized look.

Now, think of WordPress as the foundation, frame, and walls of your website, essentially taking care of the "groundwork" part of building a website. Then you (the user) can come in and customize your website in an easy-to-use interface.

That's somewhat oversimplifying it, but for the sake of this intro let's leave it at that for now.

[Note:]

For clarity, this book is all about what's called "self-hosted" WordPress, which are the files and folders you download from WordPress.org.

You may have heard of WordPress.com, but that's where you would go if you wanted WordPress (the company) to actually host your website instead of using your own hosting provider like Siteground, GoDaddy, Bluehost, etc.

If you used WordPress.com to host your website, your site's URL would look like "yourdomain.wordpress.com".

You can use WordPress.com, and even use a custom domain name with it, but you won't get complete access to all the benefits of WordPress.

However, just so there's no confusion, everything in this book is regarding "self-hosted" WordPress, not WordPress.com's website service.

[Moving on]

AT THE TIME OF THIS BOOK, WORDPRESS POWERS OVER 24% OF THE INTERNET.

When you consider there are millions of websites on the Internet, 24% is an impressive number.

Some estimate that over 74 million websites are using WordPress. These range from blogs to enterprise websites to full-blown applications.

Brands like TechCrunch, The Walking Dead, and even Forbes use WordPress in some capacity.

Check out wordpress.org/showcase/ to see more websites powered by WordPress.

It's no exaggeration to say that WordPress has quickly become the go-to resource for nearly everyone looking to start a blog or website – and for good reason.

SO THE NEXT QUESTION MOST PEOPLE HAVE IS: HOW DO YOU ACTUALLY USE WORDPRESS TO BUILD A WEBSITE?

Depending on how you came across WordPress, chances are you ended up on WordPress.org looking to download and install WordProoo, only to find that when you clicked the download button on WordPress.org, you downloaded a series of files and folders that you probably had no idea what to do with.

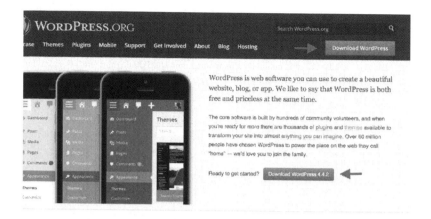

Well, in order to understand what WordPress is and how to use those files and folders, we first have to understand how websites work.

All websites on the web today have 3 basic components:

- They have a domain ("yourdomain.com")
- They have a hosting account (from a company like Bluehost, GoDaddy, or Siteground)
- They have the code of their actual website

All 3 of these things have to be "linked" together in order to get a website online.

The website code is what you provide, but you have to purchase the domain name and hosting account.

When you purchase a hosting account, you're basically renting out what's called a "server". For simplicity, let's just say a server is space on the Internet - like internet real estate.

Again, think of your website as a house.

Your hosting provider's server is the piece of land your "house" is sitting on.

Your domain is your house's address. (Except in this case we can make our "address" anything we want in order to make it easier for people to find our "house".)

Pretty simple, right?

So a website is nothing more than a bunch of code put together in files and folders, which all sit on a server that is accessible to the public (again, on a hosting provider's server like Bluehost, GoDaddy, HostGator, etc.).

The hard part of building a website is writing all the code that makes up the files and folders that make up a website. That's where WordPress comes in.

WordPress is a set of PRE-MADE files and folders that make up the foundation of a basic website, complete with everything you need to get started building and customizing your website – so you don't have to do the hard work of building every single file and folder of a website from the ground up.

WordPress is so valuable because it essentially enables anyone with a computer and a little knowledge of how WordPress works to create a great-looking website and publish regularly to that website without the help of an expensive web developer.

There are many other features and benefits to using WordPress to build your website, but for now, remember this...

WORDPRESS PROVIDES:

- The framework of your website so you don't have to write a bunch of code;
- An easy-to-use dashboard where you can make changes to your website without having to hire a developer to do it for you.

Alright, now that we know what WordPress is, we can look at how to get it installed so we can start building our website.

But first, we'll need to look at how to purchase a domain name and hosting account in order to install WordPress. That's what we'll cover in the next chapter.

02. Purchase a Domain and Hosting

Before you can jump into creating your WordPress website, you'll need to purchase a domain name (ex: myexamplebusiness.com), then purchase hosting from a company like Siteground, Bluehost, or GoDaddy.

As I mentioned in the previous chapter, think of your website as a house.

Your hosting account is the piece of land your house is built on, and your domain is your house's address.

Except in this case we can actually put any "address" (domain) we want on our "house" (website) in order to make it easier for people to find.

So the first step is to purchase a plot of land (hosting account), then slap an address on it so people know how to find it (domain).

Alright, that's enough metaphors for now. Let's look at how to purchase and setup your domain and hosting.

There are two basic ways to purchase domains and hosting:

You can purchase the domain AND hosting through the same company (like Siteground, GoDaddy, or

Bluehost). This is the least-complicated and easiest way to get started.

Or you can purchase a domain name through one company and hosting through another. This might be a better solution if you already have a domain name but no hosting account, or if you buy a domain name, then want to have hosting through another company.

For the purposes of this book, I recommend purchasing a domain and hosting with the same company. Assuming you're a complete beginner, that's the quickest and easiest way to get started, so that's the way we'll focus on first.

HERE'S HOW TO GET A DOMAIN NAME AND HOSTING ACCOUNT WITH THE SAME COMPANY (THE EASY WAY)

The first step to purchasing your domain and hosting is to actually pick a hosting provider. This is a critical decision, and picking a bad host can cause you to waste tons of time on support calls.

So how do you know which hosting company to go with? Here's how to pick a hosting provider:

SITEGROUND

Siteground is a great choice for hosting WordPress websites. Here's why:

Do a Google search for "best hosting company for WordPress" and you'll consistently see Siteground at the top of most lists. There have been a number of tests performed by various companies on the web, and Siteground has been shown to outperform the competition when it comes to uptime, site speed, support, and pretty much every other category.

Not to mention Siteground is fairly inexpensive, starting out at around $4/month for one website (I think that might be a promotional "first year" type of price, but either way it's not very expensive).

One cool thing Siteground offers that Bluehost doesn't is the option to pay for just one month starting out. After your first month, however, you'll have to purchase an annual plan (I think you can also do a quarterly plan during or after your one-month trial).

Hey, and they also give you a free domain with your new hosting account. That'll save you around $5-10 right there.

BLUEHOST

Although my recommendation usually goes with Siteground, Bluehost is still a very well-known and trusted hosting provider for WordPress sites. Like Siteground, Bluehost is also relatively inexpensive, costing around $4/month starting out for a single website.

The only thing about Bluehost is they only offer yearly plans. If you're just getting your feet wet with WordPress and websites in general, you might be a little hesitant to spend $70+ dollars on a year's worth of hosting.

The truth is, you really can't go wrong with Siteground or Bluehost. They both have great reputations and both offer great service. However, I would encourage you to do your own research, because hosting is a sensitive topic. What one person loves, another person will hate. It just comes down to individual experiences.

GoDaddy

I consider GoDaddy the "beginner on a budget" host. If you just want something cheap and simple that you can pay month-to-month, GoDaddy will work.

I used GoDaddy for years, and although they may not have the absolute best hosting on the market, they have a very clean and user-friendly layout to their website, and they offer wonderful customer service in my experience.

How to Purchase a Domain and Hosting

Okay, so once you've picked a hosting provider, it's time to make your purchase.

To purchase a domain and hosting through the same company, you'll start by going to your hosting provider of choice's website (Siteground.com, GoDaddy.com, or Bluehost.com) then clicking to go to their hosting page.

It shouldn't be difficult to find. Look in their main navigation (the one at the top of their website) and you should see something that says "Hosting" or "Web Hosting" or "Shared Hosting".

With Siteground, go to Siteground.com, then click "Web Hosting" in the top navigation, select a plan (I recommend sticking with the most basic one for now; you can always upgrade later), then you should be able to search for a domain from there.

The process is very similar with GoDaddy and Bluehost.

If you have no idea what domain you want to use, I recommend searching for an available domain before trying to purchase your hosting, that way you know which domain is available beforehand.

I typically use GoDaddy to search for available domains regardless of whether I'm going to purchase it through them or not, mainly because I like the way their search results are laid out. It really just comes down to personal preference.

Another cool service to use to find available domain names is a site called Namecheckr.com. Namecheckr not only lets you see if your domain name is available, but it also shows you if your name is taken across all major social media channels. This helps you establish cohesive branding from the very beginning.

If you're purchasing your domain and hosting through the same company, you should get the domain for free, so don't purchase your domain just yet.

Once you find an available domain, before purchasing it, head over to the "Hosting" section of your hosting provider of choice and select a plan.

Hosting plans can get complicated and frustrating to pick from, so don't overwhelm yourself right now. Most hosting providers are more than happy to upgrade your plan at any time, so don't feel like you need to purchase the whole kit-n-kaboodle right now.

Just go with what you know you need right now. Typically, that means hosting for one website with minimal extras.

You'll probably notice that many hosting companies offer "normal" hosting (or shared hosting) and "WordPress" hosting. WordPress hosting is usually more expensive and comes with features that are specifically tailored to WordPress websites.

WordPress hosting typically offers faster load times, more security, automatic updates, and more.

This may sound ideal, but I've found that WordPress hosting can be overkill for beginners with brand new websites. You're paying for extras, so it's more expensive, and you'll have stricter limits on the number of sites you can have on a WordPress hosting account.

Of course, if you have the budget and want the faster site speed, extra features, and support, go for it. Just don't think that "WordPress" hosting is a necessity for WordPress websites.

If you're just looking for something simple and inexpensive to get your started, stick with good ole shared hosting for now (that's the "regular" hosting that isn't labeled with any special term in front of it like "VPS" or "dedicated hosting").

Again, you can always upgrade at a later time if you decide you want more.

The goal right now is to not get overwhelmed.

To recap, you can't go wrong with Siteground or Bluehost, and GoDaddy works well for beginners with relatively small sites. Look at what you need right now, don't get caught up buying extras you don't need, weigh the options, then grab a hosting account and move on.

BUT WAIT, WHAT IF I ALREADY HAVE A DOMAIN, AND NOW I WANT TO PURCHASE HOSTING THROUGH ANOTHER COMPANY?

This requires changing what's called name servers. Name servers "point" your domain to your hosting account, so when people type in your domain it pulls up the right website (on the right hosting account).

To do this, you'll first need to purchase your hosting account with your new hosting company, then look for your hosting account's nameservers.

You can usually find this in your hosting account information, or in your hosting account control panel. Look for anything that says "DNS". It may actually help to hold Control (or Command on a Mac) and hit "F" to find, then search for "DNS".

It should be two number/letter combos that typically look something like this:

ns1.us10.siteground.us

ns2.us10.siteground.us

With Siteground, they're easy to find. With GoDaddy, for example, you have to do some digging.

If you're using GoDaddy, you'll have to go to your hosting account control panel, then click the "Addon Domains" link to add your domain to your hosting account (you're not purchasing it again, just telling your hosting account that you want it added).

Once you've added your domain as an addon domain, you'll then go back into your hosting account control panel and click the "DNS Manager" link. This will take you to a list of domains you've added to your hosting account.

You won't see your domain in this list. Instead, you'll have to click the "DNS" dropdown towards the top of the page, click "Manage Zones", then search for the domain you just added.

Once you've searched for your domain and found it, scroll down (or click to the next page) until you see "NS" in the "Type" column. There should be two of them, and they should look something like:

ns50.domaincontrol.com

ns51.domaincontrol.com

Those are your nameservers. Copy those down because you'll now need to go to where your domain was purchased, and change the nameservers to these two values.

BY NOW, I'M SURE YOU'RE STARTING TO SEE HOW CONFUSING POINTING AN EXISTING DOMAIN TO A NEW HOSTING PROVIDER CAN BE FOR A BEGINNER.

If you're stuck and can't figure out where your nameservers are, or what to do with them, the best thing you can do is contact your hosting provider's customer support. They should be able to help you get your domain pointed to your new hosting account. If all else fails, login to your account at Gazellish.com and send me a message. I'll be happy to help.

WHAT IF I ALREADY HAVE A HOSTING ACCOUNT, BUT WANT TO ADD A NEW DOMAIN TO IT?

Start by going to the "domains" section of your hosting provider's website and purchasing your new domain.

Once you've purchased the domain, go to your hosting account control panel (typically called cPanel, Plesk, or just a link that says "manage hosting account") and find your "Addon Domains."

Check to see if the domain name you want to use is on this list already (remember, the primary domain on your hosting account usually won't be here). If not, this is where you'll "link" your domain name to your hosting account by adding it as an addon domain.

Fill out the necessary boxes and walk through the steps on the screen to add an addon domain. This process should be pretty straight-forward.

Once you've added your new domain as an Addon Domain, the rest should be taken care of on its own. This is the beauty of having your domains and hosting with the same company. There are no extra steps for you to take in order to get everything working. Just buy a domain and add it to your hosting account as an addon domain. Easy as that.

You'll see how to install WordPress on your new domain in the next chapter, so for now you're good to go.

Okay, so now that you've purchased a domain and hosting account, you can move on to the next step. Now it's time to install WordPress so you can start building your website.

IF YOU'RE REDESIGNING AN EXISTING WEBSITE, READ THIS

If you're redesigning an existing website that is live on the web, here's what you need to know:

Chances are, you don't want to bring down your old website while you build your new one. So you're going to need to create a test site to build your new website on first, then push it live to your domain once it's completed.

To do that, I recommend going the simple route and creating a new subdomain.

Go into your hosting account's control panel (cPanel, Plesk, or just something that says "manage hosting"), then look for something that says "Subdomains".

If you're using Siteground, you would login, click "My Accounts", then click the button that says "Go to cPanel".

Once you're in your cPanel, look for the item that says "Subdomains".

I typically hold Control (or hold Command if you're on a Mac), then hit "F" to find. Then I type in "subdomain" and your browser's "find" function will find the Subdomains section for you. (Just a little shortcut I use to save time scrolling.)

Once you're in your subdomains, you're going to want to add a new subdomain.

I would make it something like "test.yourdomain.com", just to keep it simple.

Once you've created your subdomain, go back into your hosting account control panel (the one you were just in), and install WordPress on your new subdomain.

At this point, you can refer to the chapter on installing WordPress, just do so on your subdomain instead of on your actual domain.

Also, make sure you discourage search engines from indexing this test site. You can do this by going into your WordPress dashboard (after you've installed WordPress obviously), then hovering over "Settings" on the left-hand side, and clicking "Reading". Then scroll all the way down and check the box next to "Discourage search engines from indexing this site", then click "Save Changes".

Before you launch your website on your actual domain, you'll need to read the chapter on migrating a WordPress website.

But don't worry, you won't need to worry about that until your website it completed and ready to go live.

The main thing you need to know right now is:

If you're redesigning an existing website that's live on the Internet, you need to build your new WordPress website on a test site (or subdomain). We walked through how to do that by adding a new subdomain to your hosting account.

Now you can move on to the next chapter on how to install WordPress (on your test subdomain), and check out the chapter on migrating WordPress sites once you're ready to go live with your new website.

03. INSTALL WORDPRESS

Once you have your hosting account set up, it's time to install WordPress. There are basically 2 ways to install WordPress.

The easiest way is to use a WordPress installer application provided by your hosting company.

This is by far the quickest and simplest way to install WordPress in my opinion.

You'll simply log in to your hosting account and look for the link to your hosting account control panel (typically this is called cPanel, Plesk, or just a link that says "manage hosting account").

[Image]

Now look for the WordPress installer application (It should just say "WordPress" with the WordPress logo).

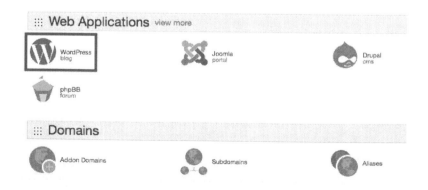

This is an application made specifically for the purpose of simplifying installing WordPress on your server.

All you have to do to install WordPress is:

- Open your WordPress installer application,
- Tell it which domain you want WordPress installed on
- Make sure the "Directory" field is left blank (don't leave "blog" in that space if it's there by default)
- Enter a user login and password
- Click install

Within a couple of minutes, it should prompt you to tell you your new WordPress install is ready to go, and you're ready to jump in and get started on your new website.

It really is as simple as that.

IF YOU MADE IT THROUGH THOSE STEPS, YOU'RE GOOD TO GO. SKIP THE REST OF THIS CHAPTER AND I'LL SEE YOU IN THE NEXT CHAPTER.

There's a more complicated way to install WordPress, and we'll go into how to do that in the rest of this chapter. However, if you're a true beginner, I recommend skipping the rest of this chapter and moving on.

However, if for whatever reason you can't use a WordPress installer app like we just described, there is another way to install WordPress. You can also use this method to install WordPress locally (on your own computer as opposed to on a hosting provider's server).

I don't recommend it for complete beginners, but if you must install WordPress yourself without an application, here's how to do it:

It involves using what's called "file transfer protocol", or FTP.

FTP is what you would use to transfer files from your computer to your public server (the one you pay for through your hosting provider). Think of this as the manual way of installing WordPress.

You would start by going to wordpress.org and downloading the WordPress files directly to your computer, then use FTP client software like FileZilla to transfer the WordPress files from your computer directly to your public server from your hosting provider.

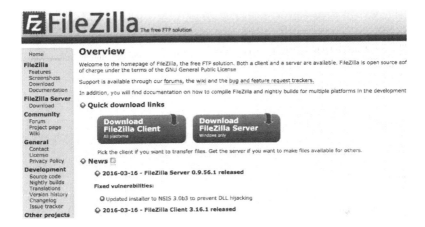

Once the files are transferred, you'll then go to your phpMyAdmin from your hosting account control panel…

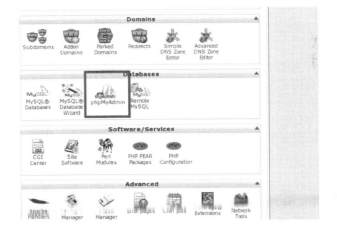

…and create a new database…

MySQL Databases

MySQL databases allow you to store a large amount of information in an easy to access manner. The dat. humans. MySQL databases are required by many web applications including some bulletin boards, conter a database, you'll need to create it. Only MySQL users (different than mail or other users) that have privi write to that database.

Create a New Database

New Database: [   ]_testdb [   ] ✓

[Create Database]

…then create a new user.

Keep up with the name of this new database and user information, because you'll need it during the WordPress install.

Next you'll need to know which folder your domain is pointing to, then upload the WordPress files to that folder.

You'll then need to navigate to your website where WordPress is actually designed to walk you through the final stages of the setup from there.

WORDPRESS

Below you should enter your database connection details. If you're not sure about these, contact your host.

Database Name	wordpress	The name of the database you want to run WP in.
User Name	username	Your MySQL username
Password	password	…and MySQL password.
Database Host	localhost	You should be able to get this info from your web host, if localhost does not work.
Table Prefix	wp_	If you want to run multiple WordPress installations in a single database, change this.

Now you just fill out the name of the database you created, the username and password you created, then you typically don't change the Database Host and Table Prefix.

Click install, and you should be good to go.

It's not too bad, and WordPress makes it as easy as possible, but it still can be a headache if you're new to all this.

If you want to know more about how to install WordPress the "manual" way, I created a video specifically for the purpose of walking through an FTP install of WordPress. To see that now, go to gazellish.com/wordpress-installation-using-ftp/.

You'll have to use your login credentials found on the very first page of this book in order to login and view it.

Having said all of that, I highly recommend NOT going the FTP route if you can help it. Not that it's bad, it just doesn't make sense to not use the installers built specifically to solve this problem for, let's say, "non-technically-inclined" people.

So, that's it. At this point you should have WordPress up and running on your website.

Now you're ready for the good part – setting up and customizing your new website. Next we'll go over what all the different aspects of WordPress do and how to use them.

04. UNDERSTANDING THE DASHBOARD

If you haven't logged in to your WordPress website, you can do so now by typing your site's domain name into the address bar in your browser, then add a "/wp-admin)" and hit enter.

You should now see a login form where you'll enter the username and password you created during the WordPress install.

Once you've logged in, you should be redirected to your WordPress dashboard. You'll see a menu on the left-hand side and several boxes on the right.

Those boxes on the right are just kind of an overhead look at your site. You'll see things like activity and news in this section.

On the left you have a list of menu items, including Dashboard, Posts, Media, Pages, etc.

For the sake of brevity, we'll just hit on the main sections you'll be interacting with the most, and we'll go more in-depth in future sections.

Most of this is pretty self-explanatory, so it shouldn't be too hard to figure out once you move around in the Dashboard a bit.

MAIN AREAS OF THE DASHBOARD

The **Posts** section is where you would create new posts, typically for a blog. Posts are usually time-stamped and can be organized into categories. There are a few other distinguishing features you should know about posts, but we'll cover that in a later chapter on Posts.

For right now, just think of posts as the place you'll create and edit blog posts.

Pages is where you'll make new pages for your site, like an About Us page or a Contact Us page. Think of pages as static or "evergreen" content that isn't time-specific and doesn't need to be categorized like posts typically do. The pages section is also where you'll make your signup pages, landing pages, and "thank you" pages as well.

Media is where all your pictures, videos, and PDFs live. You'll be able to upload them and edit them from this section. We'll talk more about that in later chapters.

Appearance is where you would go to change your theme, customize your website with WordPress's Customizer, create navigation menus, add widgets, and more. We go more in-depth into widgets in a later section in the book, so don't worry about that now.

The **Plugins** section is where you go to search for and install new plugins for your site. Think of plugins as apps. Plugins in WordPress are similar to what apps are to an iPhone or Android. Again, we have an entire chapter dedicated to understanding and using plugins, so don't get overwhelmed.

Two important sections to understand as a new WordPress user are the Tools and Settings sections.

These two can be confusing when you're first starting out, so let me explain the difference.

The **Tools** section is a place where you can import content from another WordPress site or export your site's content. When you switch domains or move your website for any reason, being able to import and export comes in handy. Honestly, you shouldn't have to use the Tools section very much.

The **Settings** section, on the other hand, is one of the most important sections of the dashboard, and it isn't always easy to understand where certain settings live.

The **General** section, under the Settings tab, is where you would change the site title and tagline (these show up in Google by default and in certain parts of some themes). You can also change your email address, time zone, language, and more.

Writing is where the settings that pertain to the writer of the posts live, and **Reading** is where the setting that affect the reader live.

Again, the naming convention isn't always intuitive, so you'll want to explore a bit in your settings to make sure you have everything the way you want.

Discussion is where you can adjust settings regarding comments, backlink notifications, your gravatar, and more.

Media (under the settings tab) is where you can adjust thumbnail sizes, although I wouldn't recommend it unless you know what you're doing.

One of the things you may want to check in your settings right now is the **Permalinks** section.

This section determines how URLs (or permalinks) show up to other people in their browser's address bar.

Under **Common Settings** you'll notice a few different options for displaying permalinks, but most modern sites go with the "Post name" setting here mainly because it makes things simpler and easier to understand, and because search engines tend to like this structure better.

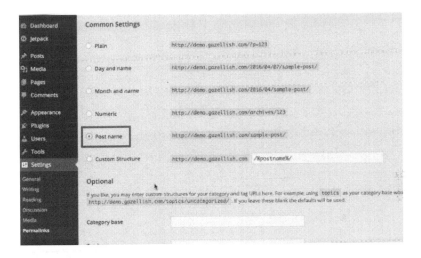

That about covers the WordPress Dashboard for now. In future chapters, we'll go in-depth into the most important aspects of each of the sections found in the WordPress Dashboard, and how to understand and use them with confidence.

And remember: The Settings section is where the options and settings for many of the plugins you install will go, so the number of items listed under this main Settings tab will grow over time. Whenever you need to know where to setting are to a new plugin, the Settings section is a great place to look first. We'll cover more about Plugins in a later chapter.

05. Adding a "Coming Soon" Page

While you're building your website, you may want to make sure the public doesn't have access to it. One way to accomplish that is by setting up a "Coming Soon" page.

We're going to do that by installing a plugin called Coming Soon Page & Maintenance Mode by SeedProd.

(Don't freak out, it's okay if you don't know what a plugin is yet. We're going to cover plugins in a much later chapter, but we need to get a "Coming Soon" page up quickly, and it's very simple to do.)

To do this, you'll need to click the "Plugins" menu item on the left-hand side of your WordPress dashboard.

Now click "Add New" at the top of the screen.

Now in the search bar in the top right, type "coming soon" and hit enter. You should see "Coming Soon Page & Maintenance Mode by SeedProd" towards the top of the list of results.

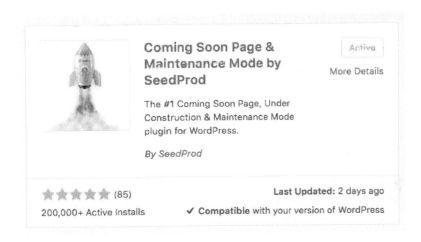

Coming Soon Page &
Maintenance Mode by
SeedProd

Active

More Details

The #1 Coming Soon Page, Under
Construction & Maintenance Mode
plugin for WordPress.

By SeedProd

★★★★★ (85)

200,000+ Active Installs

Last Updated: 2 days ago

✔ **Compatible** with your version of WordPress

It has over 200,000 installs and an average rating of 5
stars. It's simple, clean, and it has just enough
features. Let's jump in and start setting it up so you
can see for yourself.

Once we have the plugin installed, we need to head
over to the plugin's settings so we can set it up. To
get there, hover over "Settings" on the left side of the
dashboard, and click "Coming Soon Page and
Maintenance Mode".

You'll see in the top section of the settings that by
default it's disabled. You'll need to select "Enable
Coming Soon Mode" and then click "Save All
Changes".

Now scroll down a bit and you'll see that you can
upload your logo, add a headline, and add a
message. This can say whatever you want, but I
recommend something like:

Heading: Coming Soon!

Message: Our new website is coming soon. Check back later!

Then you'll probably want to include some sort of contact information, such as an email address or phone number people can reach you at in the meantime.

Now just scroll down a bit more and click "Save All Changes" and you should be all setup.

Coming Soon

Our new website is coming soon. Check back later!
In the meantime, you can reach us at johndoe@example.com.

It's going to look very simple, but that's really all you need for now. The goal is simply to keep people from seeing you build your website as you work.

If you're feeling up to it, feel free to scroll up to the top and click the "Design" tab. That's where you can change the background, text color, and more.

Don't spend too much time here though, because now it's time to start working on our website. And hey, hopefully we won't need this "Coming Soon" page up long!

06. FIND AND INSTALL A THEME

Finding and installing a theme is one of the best parts about setting up your WordPress website.

The possibilities are endless when it comes to the level of design and complexity you can find in themes nowadays, which means you can have a high-priced design on a low budget.

There are basically two routes you can take when picking a WordPress theme: free themes and premium themes.

Free themes can be found in what's called the WordPress theme directory.

To find the theme directory, go to the WordPress dashboard, then hover over Appearance and click Themes. You'll see a list of themes you currently have installed, and you can click the "Add New" button at the top to go to the theme directory.

Once you're in the theme directory, you can sort – or filter – based on colors, layout, features, and subject. To see what a theme looks like, simply click the image or click the Preview button.

Once you see one you like, just click Install, and once it's finished installing, click Activate. Now you should be able to go to your website and see your new theme.

If you've done this, you're probably wondering why your theme looks nothing like the theme demo you saw before you installed it.

Well, theme designers build out their themes with pages, posts, menus, images, and specific settings so they can showcase it better. Yours won't look exactly like theirs at first because you don't have everything set up the way they do.

Some themes are better at this than others, but sometimes the only way to get the exact look of the demo is to manually go through their code and try to spot where and how they're using widgets and plugins to get the look they have. It can be quite tedious if a theme isn't set up well out of the box.

Some themes will come with theme options you can access from the admin dashboard, or by clicking "Customize" under the Appearance tab in the admin dashboard.

Every theme is different, but the ones with good theme options make it very easy to customize the look of your site without having to go through code to figure out how a certain design was accomplished.

Every now and then you'll find a theme that makes it very easy to get started by giving you the ability to import demo content.

Themes that let you import demo content are basically giving you an exact replica of the demo version of their theme, so you can take their design and simply change out the text and images without having to do too much ground work.

Theme customization is a topic all its own, so we'll go more in-depth into that in a later section.

THE LAST THING TO LOOK AT WHEN IT COMES TO PICKING A WORDPRESS THEME IS PREMIUM THEMES.

Premium themes cost money and are sold outside of the WordPress theme directory. They tend to be higher quality, have better design, and usually come with support.

For almost every situation, I recommend using a premium theme. Free themes are nice to start out with, and can even serve as a long-term solution if they're from a reliable theme developer. But more often than not, you'll get a much better result from a premium theme.

One of my favorite premium theme companies is StudioPress. They create quality themes that are simple, clean, and very well coded.

Another great place many people go to for premium WordPress themes is Themeforest.net.

Look around ThemeForest and StudioPress, and do a few Google searches for the best premium WordPress themes. There are a TON of them on the market today, so finding a good one shouldn't be hard.

How to Install a WordPress Theme You've Purchased

Installing a premium theme is a slightly different process than installing free themes.

Once you find and purchase a premium theme, you should get a compressed, or ".zip", file from the company you purchased it from. That's the file you'll use to install your premium theme on your site.

Once that file is downloaded to your computer, go into the WordPress dashboard of your site, hover over Appearance and click Themes, then click the Add New button at the top.

Once you're there, click the Upload Theme button at the top and then click Choose File.

Find the compressed file of your theme and click Open, and then click Install Now.

Once it's installed, click the activate link and your premium theme should now be live.

Again, I highly recommend using a premium theme for almost anyone using WordPress.

They typically cost somewhere between $20 and $60, and they're well worth the money paid.

Just remember, free themes are great and they may seem like a good way to get started, but they're often designed and coded with lower standards, they're not unique, and they have a higher risk of having malicious code and spam links in them.

Alright, that pretty much covers finding and installing themes. In the next chapter, we'll take the theme you installed and start adding some content to it so we can finally start seeing how our new site is going to look.

07. CREATE PAGES AND POSTS

One slightly confusing aspect of WordPress is that you can create two different types of basic content: pages and posts.

Here's the difference between pages and posts:

POSTS

- Posts are published with time stamps,
- They're syndicated through RSS feeds (meaning people can subscribe to your posts and receive updates when you publish a new post),
- They typically include a comments section for discussion,
- They're listed in reverse chronological order on your blog,
- And perhaps most importantly, posts can be organized using categories and tags for better searchability and organization.

PAGES

Pages on the other hand, are just that: static pages.

They're:

- Not time specific
- Not syndicated through RSS feeds
- Not included in your blog feed

Pages are usually used for things like your About page or Contact page, pages that are evergreen if you will.

The page and post creation process is fairly simple…

HOW TO ADD A POST

To add a post, go to your WordPress dashboard, and click "Posts" in the menu on the left-hand side.

Now click the "Add New" button at the top.

From here you'll enter a title, then click into the text editor just below the title.

Within a couple of seconds, you should see your new post's URL appear just underneath the title you just added. You can click the "Edit" button next to this URL to change it.

Now, in the text editor (under the title and URL), you can add content to your page.

You'll notice there's a toolbar towards the top of the text editor that allows you to format your text, add links, and more, similar to ones programs like Microsoft Word use.

Look at the toolbar, and on the far right side you should see an icon that looks like a two squares on top of one another with dots inside each one.

Click that icon, and you'll see a second row of tools appear just below the first row.

The dropdown menu on the second row that says "Paragraph" is where you'll change the size of your text.

The other options in this toolbar should be pretty self-explanatory, but don't be afraid to click around to see what each button does.

In the top right, there's a box that says "Publish" at the top of it.

You'll see a "Save Draft" button and a "Preview" button at the top of this box.

You should also see things like "Status" and "Visibility" in this box, and each one should have an "Edit" link next to it.

You can change the Status to "Draft" or "Pending Review".

You can change the Visibility to "Public", "Password protected", or "Private".

In the same box, there should also be something that says "Publish immediately". This is where you can either backdate a post (make it look like it was published on an earlier date) or schedule it to post in the future.

At the bottom of this same box, there's a "Publish" button. As you could probably guess, that's where you'll publish your post once it's ready to go live. Until you click that button, no one can see your post.

Scroll down a bit on the right-hand side and you should see a box for Categories and one for Tags. We haven't created any categories or tags at this point, so you should only see "Uncategorized" under Categories - as well as an option to add categories from here - and a box where you can add tags in the Tags section.

Scroll down even more and you'll see the Featured Image box. This is where you'll add the main image of your post. Each theme decides how and when to use this featured image, so your best bet is to add a sample featured image before publishing so you can see how it will be displayed in your theme. This is also the image social networks will use when the link to this post is shared.

How to Add a Page

Adding and editing a page is very similar to adding a post. You'll click "Pages" on the left-hand side of the WordPress dashboard, then click the "Add New" button at the top.

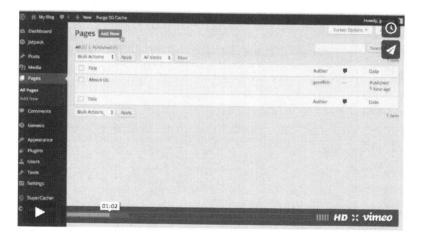

Most of the options are the same as they are with posts, except you'll notice there are no options for adding categories and tags to pages. These are only available for posts.

Another difference between pages and posts you'll probably notice is the "Page Attributes" box on the right-hand side when you're adding or editing a page.

This is where you would assign a parent page, if for example you're creating a page that will be a subpage of another on. An example of this would be if you had a Services page and you were creating a page for one of your individual services. You might want each of the services pages to fall under the main "Services" page. The URL would then look like:

yourdomain.com/services/individual-service

This same section (the "Page Attributes" section) is where you could change your page's page template.

Page templates are basically pre-made page layouts created by the theme designer for specific looks. For instance, some themes will include a "Full Width" page template that makes the page full width with no sidebar. Others will have a "Landing Page" page template that is full width, but also removes the navigation and other non-essential elements on the page in order to increase landing page conversions.

Note: If your theme doesn't have multiple page templates, then you won't see this option for page templates.

As with posts, pages can either be saved as a draft or published to the live website, and you can change the publish date to either back-date it or schedule it to publish in the future.

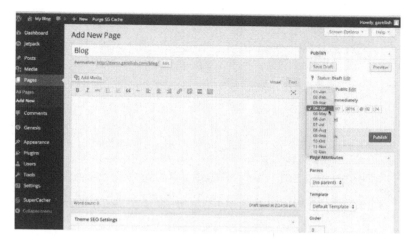

You can also change the permalink and add a featured image to pages just like you can with posts. Again, whether your page's featured image is displayed or not is determined by your theme and how it's set up.

HOW TO WRAP TEXT AROUND IMAGES IN PAGES AND POSTS

A common issue among new WordPress users is trying to figure out how to wrap text around an image.

First, add your text in the text editor. Then, click the beginning of line where you want the image to be, then click the "Add Media" button just above the text editor.

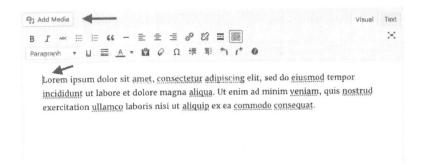

Lorem ipsum dolor sit amet, consectetur adipiscing elit, sed do eiusmod tempor incididunt ut labore et dolore magna aliqua. Ut enim ad minim veniam, quis nostrud exercitation ullamco laboris nisi ut aliquip ex ea commodo consequat.

When your image appears, it will probably be huge, so you'll want to click and drag the handle in one of the corners of the image in order to make it smaller.

Once you've sized it down appropriately, you'll now want to click the middle of the image, then in the small toolbar that pops up towards the top of the image, click the "Align right" button.

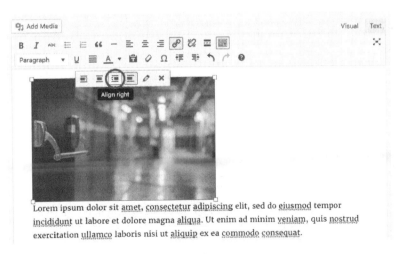

Lorem ipsum dolor sit amet, consectetur adipiscing elit, sed do eiusmod tempor incididunt ut labore et dolore magna aliqua. Ut enim ad minim veniam, quis nostrud exercitation ullamco laboris nisi ut aliquip ex ea commodo consequat.

Now you should see your image on the right, and text on the left.

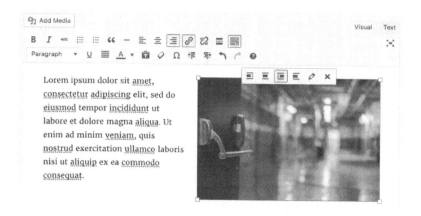

You can click the "Preview" button to see it what it looks like on your site, then click the "Publish" button to make the changes live.

Sample Page

Lorem ipsum dolor sit amet, consectetur adipiscing elit, sed do eiusmod tempor incididunt ut labore et dolore magna aliqua. Ut enim ad minim veniam, quis nostrud exercitation ullamco laboris nisi ut aliquip ex ea commodo consequat.

If you want to know how to have a "two column" layout on your page, one simple way is to use a page builder plugin. We'll cover page builder plugins in the chapter for theme customization.

HOW TO UNDO A PUBLISHED CHANGE

Don't worry, if you break anything you can't undo, just refresh your browser without saving and it should go back to the way it was before you started editing.

If you save a change and you want to undo that change, look all the way on the right-hand side, just above the "Publish" button, and you should see something that says "Revisions:" with a number beside it.

Click the "Browse" link on the same line, and you'll see the history of revisions made to this post or page. You can click the "Previous" button in the top left to revert back to the most recent version.

When you find the version you want to revert back to, click the "Restore This Revision" button, and your post or page will be taken back to that version.

ASSIGNING HOME AND BLOG PAGES

Once you've created a couple of pages, we now need to tell WordPress which page does what.

Start by going to your Settings and clicking Reading. This is where you can select which page you want to be your home page and which one you want to be your blog page.

By default, "your latest posts" is selected next to the "Front page displays" setting. This setting will essentially make your homepage the place where your blog feed shows up.

To change this, simply select "static page" and tell WordPress which page you want to be your homepage and which one you want to be your blog page. If you don't want to set up a blog for your site, leave the "Posts page" setting blank and click save.

It's important to note that some themes have it set up to where their homepage is pre-built and customizable through either their theme settings or by adding widgets to special home page widget areas.

If this is the case, you'll probably want to make sure "Your latest posts" is selected.

This might not make sense to you now, but that's okay. It has to do with how some theme designers choose to set up their individual theme's template files, or the files that make up a WordPress site. We'll cover template files in a much later section, so don't worry about that for now.

08. CREATE CATEGORIES AND TAGS

One of the more valuable features of WordPress is its ability to organize website content with taxonomies.

WordPress has 4 default taxonomies, but we're only going to cover the 2 most relevant: categories and tags.

In a previous chapter, we talked about the difference between pages and posts, and how one of the main differences is the ability to organize posts using categories and tags.

In this chapter, we're going to go more in-depth into how to use categories and tags in your WordPress site and why they're important.

Let's start with why you even need categories and tags.

TechCrunch.com is a great example of how categories can be used in WordPress.

Their site is using WordPress, and you can see how each of the sections in their navigation correspond with a category on their site. So when you click on one of their categories, you see a feed of posts that are tagged as being a part of that category.

Tags are a little bit harder to find, but it looks like on the left hand side they have tags for each of their posts as well.

Each post can have multiple categories and multiple tags.

Aside from the fact that categories and tags make browsing a website much easier, search engines love when sites are structured this way. It helps them crawl the site better, and it helps improve the user's experience, which is the ultimate goal of search engines.

Now let's look at how we can incorporate categories and tags into our WordPress site.

CREATING CATEGORIES

Start by hovering over Posts, and clicking Categories.

Enter the name of your category and click Add New Category.

Create a couple so we can see how it all works, then once you have a few categories, let's look at tags.

CREATING TAGS

There are two ways to add tags. One way is to hover over Posts and click Tags, then add tags the same way we added categories.

The other way is to add tags while you're editing a post. This makes it easier to add tags as you're writing your content and it's fresh on your mind.

Go ahead and add a post now so you can see how to add categories and tags to individual posts:

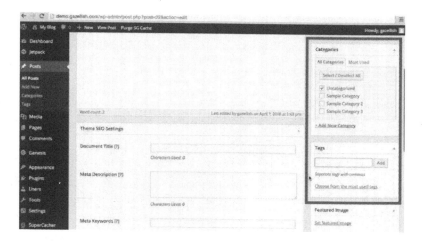

Now that we're inside the post, we can see that the categories we added are now on the right hand side, and there's also a text box where we can add tags if we want. (See above)

All we have to do is add the categories and tags we want and then click update and it's done.

Now how can we see our category pages and add them to our menu, like TechCrunch did?

Well, we can go directly to our category page (or link people to our category page) by typing in our domain name followed by a "/category/(slug of our category)".

If you don't remember the slug of a category, simply go back into your dashboard to where the categories are and click View.

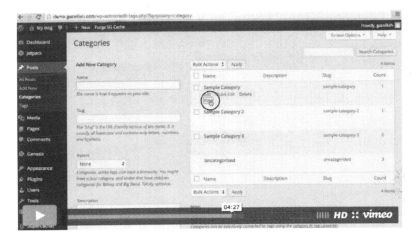

You'll see the URL in the address bar.

To add categories to our navigation as menu items, we just go to our Menus, under Appearance, and click the Categories drop-down on the left hand side. Select your categories and click Add to Menu.

Now people will be able to go directly to our category pages from our menu.

ONE LAST THING ON CATEGORIES.

Categories can be nested under parent categories. For example, if I wanted to make a category called "Events" and I wanted a subcategory called "Summer Events" I would create an Events category, and then create a category called "Summer Events" and specify Events as its parent category.

Now any time you put a post in the "Summer Events" category, it'll show up on the Summer Events category page AND the Events category page, even though you didn't specify it as being in the Events category – because Summer Events is now a sub-category of Events.

That about covers the basics of categories for now. In the next section, we're going to learn what Widgets are and how to use them.

09. CREATE NAVIGATION MENUS

Now that we have a couple of pages to work with, we need to create a menu for our site.

To do this, hover over Appearance and click Menus.

From here you simply type in the name of your new menu you want to create, then click the "create menu" button.

Now you can start adding items to your menu.

You'll notice on the left-hand side that you can use pages, posts, categories, or custom links to add to your menu. Just check the boxes next to the pages or categories you want to add to your menu, then click the "Add to Menu" button.

Once they're added to your menu, you can click and drag the items to change their order.

Most of this is fairly self-explanatory, but there are two things we should go over about menus.

THE FIRST THING IS NESTED MENU ITEMS, OR SUB-MENUS.

A sub-menu is a menu nested within a menu item. A good example of this would be if you had a category menu item, and wanted to put the sub-categories of that category as a menu nested within that menu item.

That sounds really confusing, but here's what I mean:

You see these everywhere, and chances are you'll want to do this at some point.

To accomplish this in WordPress, simply add all of your sub-menu items to your menu, then click and drag the sub-menu items slightly to the right underneath whichever menu item you want them to be nested under.

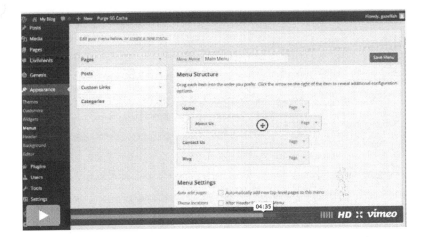

All of the nested menu items that belong in the same sub-menu should be aligned, and all of the ones you want nested further in the menu should be just to the right of their "parent" menu item.

Now when you save and refresh, you'll see that the nested menu items you added only show up when you hover over their parent menu item.

THE SECOND THING WE NEED TO COVER IS CUSTOM LINKS.

Let's say, for example, you want to create a menu item called "Services".

Then you want to add sub-menu items for each of the services you offer.

Now let's say that for whatever reason you don't have an actual "Services" page that lists all of your services. Instead, you have landing pages for each of your services, and you'd like to send visitors directly to the landing page for the service they're interested in.

To do this, you'll need to add a custom link to your menu with the link text of "Services". The URL can't be empty, so either put "/" or "#" for now.

As soon as you add the menu item, click it so you can edit it, then delete the URL and click save.

Now you'll have a menu item that isn't a link, but instead is only a parent menu item that leads visitors to the correct sub-menu item (which are services in this case).

ALRIGHT, ONE LAST STEP TO CREATING A MENU:

This is important, because if you skip this step you'll be stuck wondering how to make your menus show up on your site.

You'll notice under Menu Settings there's a thing called "Theme locations".

These are the locations set up by your individual theme, and checking one of these boxes tells your theme to place this menu in that location.

If you don't assign a menu location to your menu, it won't show up anywhere on your website (unless of course you use a menu widget and place it in a widget area, but that's a different story).

Theme developers create certain locations in their theme where menus can be displayed. Common locations included the header and footer, but some theme developers get creative from time to time.

Most of the time the main menu location (typically in the header) will be the "Primary" menu location.

You will see themes that have a location for a "secondary" menu or "footer" menu, and you'll just have to play around with assigning menus to those locations to see where they show up. When in doubt, just assign a menu to a location, save, then refresh your site to see where it showed up.

Every theme is different, but it usually doesn't take long to figure out where the menu locations are.

NOW, BEFORE WE CLOSE THE CHAPTER OUT, THERE'S ONE LITTLE MENU-HACK YOU MIGHT NEED TO KNOW ABOUT.

If it's too much for right now, you can always refer back to it later.

Let's say you want to show certain menu items only in certain situations, like when visitors are on certain pages, logged in, etc.

There's a cool plugin called Menu Item Visibility Control (wordpress.org/plugins/menu-items-visibility-control/) that lets you specify when each menu item should display or be hidden.

Once it's installed, go to Menu under Appearance (like normal), but this time you can click on a menu item and you'll see that it has a visibility option now.

This part's a little tricky, because you'll need to know a little bit of "WordPress language" to use this. We'll have to use what WordPress calls "conditional tags", but don't worry, there's an entire list of them at codex.wordpress.org/Conditional_Tags.

It might look like gibberish at first, but it's actually very easy to understand.

For example, let's say you only want the "Home" menu item to appear whenever visitors are NOT on your home page. Makes sense right?

To do that, you would click on the "Home" menu item, and in the "visibility" input, you would put:

! is_front_page()

The "is_front_page()" is a conditional that checks to see if it's the home page, and the "!" just means "not".

So "! is_front_page()" means "if the page is not home".

Now that menu item will only display if the page being displayed is not the home page.

You can get pretty creative with this, and it actually makes for a very dynamic and useful site.

Another great use for this would be if you wanted to display a list of blog categories when users are on your Blog page. So anywhere else on the site, you would want to hide all of the categories, but on the Blog page, have them visible. That way when people show interest in the blog by visiting it, they'll get more of that type of content in the navigation.

Conditionals for the blog are a little less intuitive, but you can use the "is_home()" conditional to check to see if the user is on the blog page. You might think "is_home()" would be used to identify the home page, but that's actually what "is_front_page()" is used for.

So here's what you would use to make other menu items disappear when on the blog page.

! is_home()

Alright, let's take it one step further and then we're done.

Let's say you want to remove every menu item EXCEPT the Contact page link whenever someone navigates to your pricing page. Whether this is a good idea or not is a whole different conversation. Let's just pretend you want to try it out to see if it works.

To do this, you would need a conditional that only shows menu items whenever visitors are NOT on the pricing page. Here's what your conditional tag would look like to accomplish that:

is_page('pricing-page')

With that conditional, you can see that it's checking to see if it's a page, and if that page has a "slug" (think "URL") of pricing-page. In other words, if the URL is yoursitedomain.com/pricing-page.

Obviously, you would replace the 'pricing-page' with your pricing page's slug (the last part of the URL).

Here's where you can find the conditional tags for pages:

developer.wordpress.org/reference/functions/is_page/

One of the beautiful things about WordPress is you can Google almost any problem you have and find an answer. WordPress has such a strong community, there aren't many questions that haven't been answered several times.

If you get lost or want to try something that isn't easy to find, try Googling "WordPress is ___" and insert the conditional you want to check for in the place of the blank.

Okay, so that was the long way around menus, but now you should be able to create menus and sub-menus, place your menus in menu locations so they actually show up on your site, and you can even make certain menu items show or hide based on what visitors are doing on your site.

10. How to Use Widgets and Sidebars

Every WordPress theme has what's called "widget areas". These widget areas are sometimes referred to as "sidebars", but they're one in the same.

Widget areas are areas that are designed to display widgets – which are basically just blocks of content that display added features on your website.

Think of it like this:

Your phone has apps that do different things, right? You may have an app for taking notes, an app for Facebook, an app that displays pictures, etc.

Well, think of widgets as little "apps" for your website. Each widget does something different, and each one has a purpose. For instance, there are text widgets for displaying text, widgets for displaying a list of categories, widgets to display your recent posts, and much, much more.

But these widgets (or "apps") can only be placed on your website in certain areas - areas the theme developer created specifically for widgets to be displayed. These are called "widget areas".

You can put any widget you want in these widget areas, but you can't change where the widget areas are in your theme (at least not without having some coding knowledge).

Let's look at how to add widgets to your theme's widget areas.

ADDING WIDGETS TO WIDGET AREAS

To find your widgets, hover over Appearance and click Widgets.

As you can see, WordPress comes with certain default widgets, like search, text, pages, categories, and more.

To add a widget to a widget area, all you do is click and drag.

You can also click a widget, then select the widget area you want to add it to, then click Add Widget.

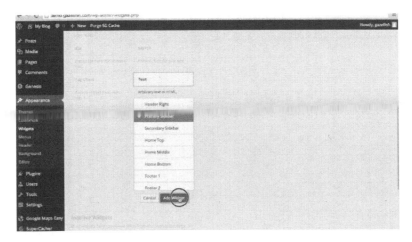

Once the widget is in a widget area, you'll then see settings for it. (You may have to click it in order to see it's settings.)

Not all widgets have settings, but they do all have a title, which isn't required. Once your widget is in a widget area, you should be able to go to your website and see it displayed. There is no traditional "Publish" or "Save" button, other than the save buttons that are in each individual widget.

One thing that confuses new WordPress users is this idea of where widget areas are located in the theme and how to move them. We touched on it at the beginning of this chapter, but it's worth mentioning again.

Every theme has different widget areas in different places, depending on how the theme was built. There is no way by default in WordPress to move a widget area without altering the code of the theme.

Theme developers will look at their theme and say, "This is a place where someone might want to add or remove content," like a search bar or a contact form or recent posts, so they'll create a widget area and place it in that location.

I'll stress this again, because many WordPress beginners tend to get confused by widgets:

Think of widgets to your websites like apps are to a phone, and widget areas are just places to show off your "apps".

We use the app metaphor with plugins too, but like we'll mention in the plugins chapter, that's because plugins can function as widgets.

This is another slightly confusing part of WordPress, but think of widgets and plugins like this:

WordPress comes with default widgets (search, text, etc.). These only exist as widgets, which means they can only be displayed in widget areas and can't be used any other way.

However, you can download PLUGINS to add extra functionality to your WordPress site, then if it's a plugin that comes as a widget, you can use that plugin's WIDGET as one way to display it in WIDGET AREAS.

If that lost you, don't worry. There's a LOT more to learn about plugins, and we have an entire chapter dedicated to plugins later in the book.

For now, just remember that widgets are added to widget areas to display "apps" (default widgets and downloaded plugins) that add functionality to your site.

NOW LET'S TIE IT ALL TOGETHER BY LOOKING AT HOW TO CREATE AND CUSTOMIZE SIDEBARS ON OUR SITE.

Remember how we said that widget areas are sometimes called sidebars? Well that's because sidebars on a WordPress website are typically made up of widgets.

So what if we want to make a different sidebar for different sections of our site? For example, what if we want our Contact page sidebar to be different than our Blog sidebar?

Well, there's a neat plugin that lets you build and customize sidebars for different pages on your site. It's called Custom Sidebars.

In the context of this plugin, sidebars are referring to any widget area, so they don't actually have to be on the side of the page. They can be in the footer or header, or anywhere else your theme has a widget area for that matter.

To show how this plugin works, we'll create a "Blog" sidebar and a "Contact Page" sidebar…

Now we need to open the editor of those pages, then on the right-hand side we'll see the option to select a different sidebar for this page.

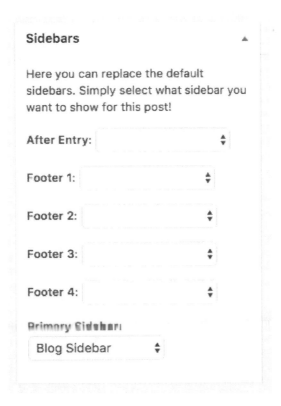

We'll select the sidebar we want to replace our standard one, then click save. Now our new sidebar will show up only on this page.

We can also do the same thing to display different sidebars for certain categories, or for certain post types.

You'll probably come up with a million different ways to create and customize your sidebars, so feel free to explore and make as many changes as you need. WordPress makes moving widgets around in widget areas unbelievably simple, with just a click and a drag.

And if you want to move a widget out of a sidebar or widget area without deleting it altogether, simply drag it down to the "Inactive Widgets" section on the left-hand side of the Widgets page, just below all your widgets.

That's about it for widgets. Now that we understand widgets and sidebars, it's time to learn more about plugins in the next chapter.

11. How to Use Plugins

Plugins are one of the most useful features of WordPress.

WordPress.org defines plugins as "…ways to extend and add to the functionality that already exists in WordPress."

As you saw when we covered widgets, that's very similar to how we explained widgets as well. It's important to understand the relationship between plugins and widgets, because they're so closely related.

Plugins for WordPress are similar to what apps are for a phone. We say that about widgets too because plugins and widgets are essentially one in the same.

Think of widgets as one way to display or use a plugin.

It's a little more complicated than that, but for simplicity, it's better for now if you think of widgets as tools you can use to display plugins and added features.

Here's another way to think about it:

To get a new plugin on your site, you have to download and install it, similar to how you would for an app.

Once a plugin is installed (depending on what type of plugin it is) there are usually 2 ways to display plugins - or use plugins - on your site.

One way is to use what's called a shortcode, which looks like this:

[example-shortcode]

Plugins that use shortcodes will typically come with them so you can copy and paste without having to worry about messing anything up.

Another way to use a plugin is to use the plugin's widget, and put it in one of your theme's widget areas.

If you're still confused, here's an example:

Let's say you want a contact form in your sidebar.

Well, after poking around our theme a bit, we know that our sidebar is one of our theme's widget areas, so, we go to our widgets to see if maybe there's a contact form we can put in there.

As you'll probably see, there isn't a widget for a contact form, so we're going to need to "add functionality to our WordPress site" – which is the definition of a plugin.

So let's see if we can find a plugin for this.

We'll click Plugins in the left hand side in the dashboard and we'll see a list of plugins we have currently installed.

You may be wondering what these plugins are, but don't worry about that for now. For now, we're just going to click Add New at the top and we're taken to the plugin repository.

The WordPress Plugin repository is similar to the theme directory, but for plugins. All plugins in this area are free, just like themes, and the install process is similar too.

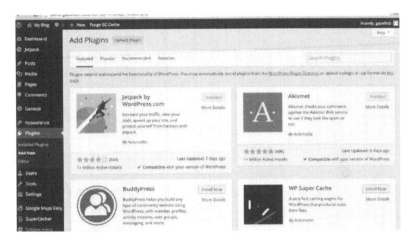

To find what we need, we're going to search for "contact form" in the search bar and hit enter.

You'll see a long list of contact form plugins, but in this instance let's say I've done some research on the web and found one particular contact form plugin that has a lot of good reviews.

It's called Contact Form 7, so I'm going to search for that specific name and hit enter.

Now, if we want to read more about it and how to use it, we can click More Details.

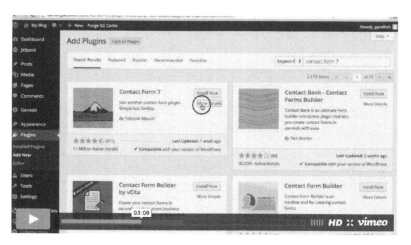

This is important, because it's one of the most confusing things about plugins:

Remember how I said that plugins are typically displayed or used in one of two ways: using the plugin's widget or using its shortcode?

Well, oftentimes you're going to have to use a shortcode to display or use your plugin, and each plugin's shortcode is found in a different place depending on the plugin's developer.

Some plugins will have the shortcode you need to use sitting under the description section of the plugin details, seen here...

…while other plugins may have it under the Installation section, here:

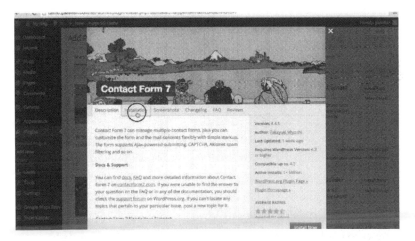

Some plugins, like Contact Form 7, give you the shortcode you need to use after you've created a form, so we won't see it here.

Shortcodes can be frustrating to find, but remember, to display your plugin (or use your plugin), more often than not, you have to have either a shortcode or a widget.

There is an exception to this, but we'll talk about that at the end of this section.

For now, let's install Contact Form 7 so we can see how it works.

Now that we've installed the plugin, where do we find it so we can start using it?

This is another confusing part about WordPress plugins:

EVERY PLUGIN CAN SHOW UP IN A DIFFERENT PLACE IN YOUR WORDPRESS DASHBOARD – IT COMPLETELY DEPENDS ON THE PLUGIN'S DEVELOPER.

Some plugin developers will put their plugin's dashboard (or settings) under the Settings tab. Some will put it under the Tools tab, some will only put it in as a widget, and some will create a completely new tab altogether for their plugin.

Sometimes it takes some looking around, but just know that when you install a plugin, that plugin's dashboard or settings section won't necessarily go to one particular place in your dashboard.

It looks like this plugin has created its own tab in our WordPress Dashboard navigation, which makes it easy to find.

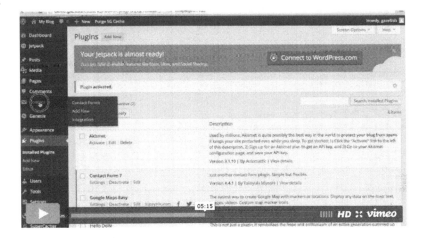

Now go into the Contact Form 7 plugin, click Add New at the top to create a new form, create a simple form, then click Save.

The settings used to create a new form are outside of the scope of this section, but good plugin developers will give you instructions on how to use their plugin. You'll just have to go into Plugins and click View Details to see instructions.

With this particular plugin, now that we've created a form, we can see that it gives us our shortcode to use in order to display it.

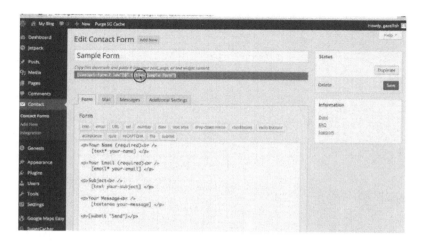

We can use this shortcode anywhere we have a text editor on our site.

So for example, you can copy the shortcode, head over to your Widgets section, drag a text widget into the Primary Sidebar, then paste the shortcode in and click Save.

Now when we go to our site and click refresh, we see our new contact form displaying.

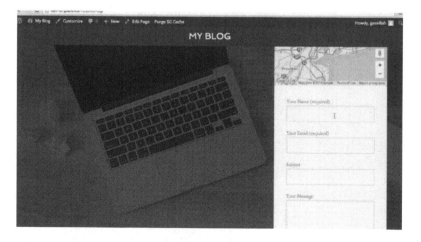

With this plugin, the shortcode was easy to find, but not all plugins make it easy to find their shortcode.

You'll likely have to do some searching to find the shortcode for some plugins, and other plugins won't have shortcodes at all, it just depends on the purpose and use of the plugin.

When in doubt, it never hurts to Google the name of the plugin followed by "shortcode" and you'll likely find someone else asking the same question.

NOW, ONE MORE THING BEFORE WE WRAP UP.

Remember how we said that MOST plugins use shortcodes and widgets to display on your site? Well there is an exception.

See, not all plugins CAN be displayed on your site.

Some plugins are created to simply solve a problem, and there is no way to display them.

There should still be a settings section for most plugins you install, and those will show up somewhere in your WordPress Dashboard like we talked about earlier, but not all plugins are meant to be displayed.

This is an important point because it helps you understand what a plugin actually is.

Remember, plugins ADD FUNCTIONALITY to your site.

That could be a contact form, or it could just be a plugin that speeds up your site's load time – in which case there's nothing to really do other than tweak the plugin's settings a bit and make sure it's activated.

Think of it this way: let's say you're running your WordPress site when you come to a problem you need solved.

Maybe it's that your site is running slowly or maybe you just need security so your site doesn't get hacked. Without WordPress, you would likely have to hire a developer to write custom code to add these features to your site.

Well, with WordPress, that's what plugins are for – it's like a pre-packaged solution built by a developer that can be free or cost money.

That's right, just like themes, you can also buy premium plugins by going to sites like CodeCanyon.net or by simply Googling "WordPress plugin for _____".

This, in my opinion, is what makes WordPress so great: the ability to do almost anything you want with your website without paying thousands of dollars to a developer to build it. All you have to do (in most cases) is find the right plugin!

Alright, that was a lot to take in for anyone new to WordPress.

I would encourage you to search around on the Internet for things like "best plugins for a new WordPress website" and look around the WordPress plugin repository as well so you can really see the types of things plugins can do.

12. CREATE A CONTACT FORM

We're going to use a well-known contact form plugin (from the previous chapter) called <u>Contact Form 7</u>.

If you just read the previous chapter, you should already have it installed.

First, let me say this. There are a ton of contact form plugins out there for WordPress, so please feel free to look around and try a few different ones. I've just always had good experiences with Contact Form 7, and it's one of the most popular WordPress plugins ever, so that's the one we'll use in this chapter.

Contact Form 7 is also free to use, so we'll go ahead and install it, then activate it (if you haven't already).

For this demo, I'm going to pretend that we're using MailChimp for our email marketing, and I'm going to search for the <u>MailChimp extension plugin for Contact Form 7</u>.

If you use a different email marketing service, or if you'd rather not worry about email marketing at this time, there's no need to install this plugin.

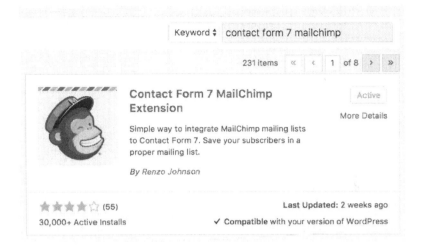

Keyword ⬍   contact form 7 mailchimp

231 items   «   ‹   1   of 8   ›   »

Contact Form 7 MailChimp Extension   Active

More Details

Simple way to integrate MailChimp mailing lists to Contact Form 7. Save your subscribers in a proper mailing list.

By Renzo Johnson

★★★★☆ (55)   Last Updated: 2 weeks ago

30,000+ Active Installs   ✓ Compatible with your version of WordPress

This plugin essentially makes it so that whenever someone fills out a form on your site, they're automatically added to one of your MailChimp lists.

Now that we have both Contact Form plugins installed, we'll need to create our first form.

On the left hand side of the dashboard, click on the Contact link. At the very top, click Add New, then give your form a name, and click Save.

You can add fields by clicking one of the buttons (below), and you'll notice this plugin gives you a shortcode for each field you add.

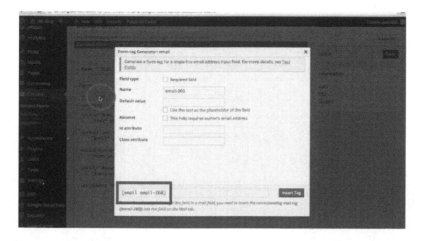

You'll probably notice there are HTML tags wrapped around the default form fields in Contact Form 7 that look like "<label>" or "<p>".

You can use their default code as a guide if you want, and you can copy/paste their code then replace the necessary text with your own.

You can also simply leave the HTML out if it becomes too confusing. I recommend including it as it helps format the form correctly, but if something breaks due to misplaced code, you can resort to simply including the fields themselves without the HTML code wrapped around them.

Once you have a few fields in your form, you can go ahead and link your form to your MailChimp account (if you don't have one, it's free to sign up at mailchimp.com).

Again, this part is completely optional. If you'd rather not worry about email marketing right now, or if you use a different email marketing service, feel free to skip to where it says "Now we need to put our form on our site".

Click the MailChimp tab from within the form editor, and you'll notice there are four fields we need to fill out. The first two are the Name and Email fields, where we'll copy and paste the shortcodes from the Form tab.

You'll have to get the last two fields from your MailChimp account.

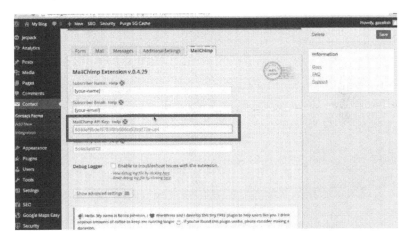

To do that, login to your MailChimp account, click on the user name at the top, and click Account. Then click Extras > then API keys > then click Create a Key. Then copy and paste the API key into your contact form's field.

The last thing to do in MailChimp is go into Lists and next to the list you want to use, click the dropdown arrow and click Settings.

Now scroll all the way down and you'll see the List ID, which we'll copy and paste into the last field of our contact form's MailChimp extension. Now scroll down and click Save, and we're ready to put our form on our site.

NOW WE NEED TO PUT OUR FORM ON OUR SITE

All that's left to do now is:

- Copy the shortcode for our new form,
- head into our Widgets section,
- add a text widget to one of our widget areas,
- and paste the form's shortcode.

Now click save, and we should be able to see our new form live on our site. And if you try it out, you should see that you're now added to MailChimp once you submit a form.

One last thing about Contact Form 7:

If you want people to be redirected to a Thank You page after they submit a form, you'll have to go back in to edit your form, and click the Additional Settings tab.

This part's not quite as intuitive as it should be, so let me help you out a bit.

The code you'll want to put here in order to redirect someone to a Thank You page after submission, is this:

on_sent_ok: "location = 'http://yourdomain.com/';"

Now click Save, and you should be good to go.

By now you should have a basic contact form live on your website.

13. SECURE YOUR SITE

WordPress security might not be the most exciting topic, but it's definitely one of the most important.

Think about it from a hacker's perspective:

- WordPress is the most popular CMS in the world right now – so there are literally tons of websites to target,
- WordPress is open source – meaning the code's available to anyone online,
- and pretty much all WordPress websites use third-party themes and plugins – which add even more security vulnerabilities.

With all that in mind, it's smart to think about security early, so you don't have to stress when it's too late.

After all, if a hacker can find just one vulnerability in a single theme or plugin you have installed, whether it's active or not, he or she can usually get into your server and cause irreparable damage.

Now that we understand the importance of security for our WordPress site, let's look at a few basics things we can do to make our site more secure.

For starters, ALWAYS make sure you update both your WordPress install and the themes and plugins you have installed.

Out-of-date themes, plugins, and WordPress installs give hackers an opportunity to exploit older vulnerabilities.

To see if you have any available updates, go to your WordPress dashboard and click Updates under the Dashboard tab.

If you're running an old version of WordPress or if you have any plugins that need to be updated, you'll be able to see them and update them from here.

Another thing you can do to make your site more secure is make sure you don't have a user named "admin".

This is common for new WordPress sites, but it makes it that much easier for hackers when they already know your username. All they have to do at that point is guess your password. Which leads us to the next point…

Don't use basic or generic passwords.

Make sure your password is at least 8 to 10 characters with upper and lower case letters, numbers, and special characters if you can.

The next thing to think about when it comes to WordPress security is, you want to **make sure you're using as few plugins as possible, and only use trusted, popular themes**.

As we've mentioned before, every plugin you install is another opportunity for hackers, so get rid of any plugins you have installed that are either:

a) Not being using,
b) Aren't activated, or
c) Simply aren't serving much of a purpose.

You also want to make sure you backup your website regularly in case you ever need to restore it.

BackupBuddy is a well-known plugin for this, but feel free to do some research to find one you like.

Lastly, you'll want to find a good plugin for general WordPress security.

Two of the main ones I've found are Wordfence and iThemes Security.

These plugins have a lot of features, but they're still fairly easy-to-use. Check out each of these to see which you prefer, and then go through the plugin's startup guide once you have one installed so you make sure you're using it properly.

I'm going to use iThemes Security for this example, and once it's installed you'll see that there's a button that says "Secure Your Site Now".

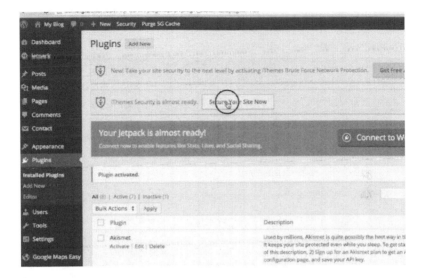

When we click that, we see 4 more buttons that make it very easy for us to get setup quickly with basic configurations.

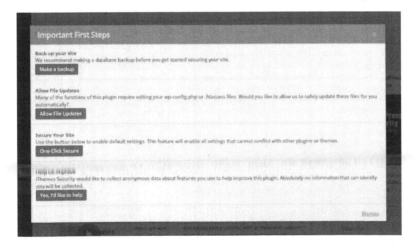

Well, that's about it for WordPress security for right now.

There are MANY more things you can do to improve your website's security, and your website will never be 100% secure, but if you do the things we've talked about in this chapter, you'll be well ahead of most other WordPress websites on the web today. You'll also have taken a huge step toward preventing your WordPress website from getting hacked.

14. Set Up Analytics

One of the most important things you can do before launching your website is get Google Analytics set up.

Google Analytics is free to use and gives you a ton of data on your website's visitors. It shows you things like:

- Where your website visitors are coming from
- Which pages your visitors are looking at the most
- Which pages they're leaving your website on
- What your website's conversion rates are
- And a WHOLE bunch more

It's actually amazing that Google provides this level of insight for free. And you need to have your website linked up to Google Analytics from day one. Here's how to do it.

How to Link Your WordPress Website to Google Analytics

To start, you'll need a Google Analytics account. Go to analytics.google.com and go through the steps to create an account.

At some point in the account creation process, you should see something that says "Tracking Code". It'll start with "<script>" and end with "</script>". Highlight this code, then hold Control (or Command on a Mac) and hit "C" to copy the code.

Now head back over to the WordPress dashboard of your site. Now hover over Plugins, and click "Add New".

You don't have to use a plugin to link your website to your Google Analytics account, but we're going to in this book so you don't get lost trying to add code to your theme's template files.

The plugin we're going to use is called "Insert Headers and Footers" (the URL is wordpress.org/plugins/insert-headers-and-footers/) from WPBeginner.

Once it's installed and activated, hover over "Settings" in the main menu on the left-hand side of the WordPress dashboard, then click "Insert Headers and Footers".

You should now see 2 boxes: one that says "Scripts in Header" and another that says "Scripts in Footer".

Paste the tracking code you got from your Google Analytics account into the box that says "Scripts in Header" and click "Save".

HOW TO TEST YOUR GOOGLE ANALYTICS TRACKING CODE

Once you've installed the tracking code in your header, give Google Analytics a little time to catch up. This could take as much as a day or so, so be patient.

Here's how Google says to see if your tracking code is working:

Sign in to your Analytics account, then select the property and "view" you set up for your website. If you recently added the tracking code, you'll probably only have one "view".

Now go to the Reporting tab, then select Real-Time > Overview.

This is where you'll be able to see traffic on your website in real-time.

In another tab, pull up your website, then leave that tab open and go back to the Google Analytics tab you just pulled up.

You should see the words "Right now" with a number underneath it.

If that number is at least "1", then you did it! That means Google Analytics is picking up at least one visitor on your site, so the tracking code is reading properly.

If you're still seeing a "0", wait a while then try again.

If you can't get Google Analytics to show any traffic on your site after you've waited at least 24 hours, you can:

- Check the source code of your site by right-clicking (or holding Control and clicking on a Mac) anywhere on your website, then clicking "View Page Source". It may say something different if you're not using Chrome, but either way it'll say something along the lines of "View Source". Once you're looking at the source code, hold control (or hold Command on a Mac) and hit "F" to find. I usually search for the word "Google" or "UA-".
- Go to gachecker.com and enter your domain name. They'll tell you whether or not your Google Analytics tracking code is installed. I don't vouch for this site's legitimacy, but I can say they've been accurate for me in the past.

If you still can't get your Google Analytics tracking code setup properly, login to your account at Gazellish.com and start a topic in the support forum. I'll try to jump in to help you troubleshoot so you can get Google Analytics setup on your site quickly.

15. CUSTOMIZE YOUR THEME

Anyone who's used WordPress for more than 2 minutes typically wants to know, how do I change the colors and the fonts, and how do I add my logo, or add a background color, etc.?

Well in this section we're going to learn how to do just that – how to customize your WordPress website.

Let's start with the basics.

WordPress gives you a way to customize the very basic aspects of your website with their default customizer. To get to it, all you do is hover over Appearance and click Customize.

You'll be taken to a page where you'll see your website on the right hand side and a menu on the left.

The Site Identity section is where you can change the title and tagline of your site, and you'll also see some familiar items like Menus, Widgets, and Static Front Page. We can also add a logo to our site in the Header Image section.

The rest of the items in this menu are what we can use to customize the basic look of our site.

As you can see, your options are fairly limited when it comes to what all you can customize by default in WordPress.

Theme developers are really the ones who decide what all should be customizable in their themes, so every theme is different.

You'll notice that the Customizer has more or less options depending on which theme you have installed.

Most premium themes come with a complete set of options within their theme settings that allow you to change almost anything you want. More popular themes like Avada and themes from Themify tend to have tons of options so you can make your website look the way you want without writing any code or installing extra plugins.

Unfortunately, in this case, we're working with a theme that doesn't really give us many options for customization, so we're going to need to look for a plugin to help us out.

A good plugin I've come across in the past for basic theme customization is called Customify, but you're welcome to do some searching on your own to find the best one.

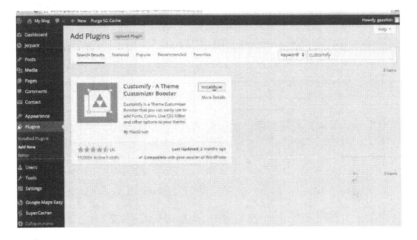

It might be worth looking around to find one you can buy that includes support, that way you know you have someone to help if you need it.

However, if you want to use a free plugin, Customify seemed pretty good, so I'm going to install it, activate it, and head to my Customizer.

(In this case I just happen to know that the Customizer is where this plugin puts its options.)

In the Customizer we can see that our plugin has added some options to the default customizer that allow us to change the fonts (using Google Fonts) and colors of our website.

Let's make a few basic changes so we can see how it works…then we'll hit Save & Publish…and now let's close the customizer so we can see our changes on our live site.

And there we go, as you can see, our changes are now live.

Now, you may be thinking, colors and fonts are cool but how do I change the actual layout of my website?

Well, your website's layout is determined by the theme you're using, so changing the location of the header or sidebars, for instance, would all depend on whether or not your theme gives you the option to change that.

Even though you can't necessarily change the layout of your entire website without help from your theme's options, you can use plugins to change the layout of individual pages.

Let's say for instance you want to build a page, like a Contact page, but you can't seem to get the layout the way you want it to look.

Well, there's a plugin for that.

Before we install a plugin though, there's an important thing to know about page layouts in WordPress.

Every theme has a certain number of pre-built page layouts, called page templates.

If you create or edit a page, on the right hand side you should (for most themes) see a drop-down with the word "Template" above it.

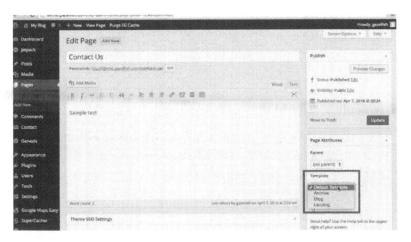

This shows you which page template this page is using, and you can also change it to any other page template the theme developer has set up.

Typically, theme developers will create at least a few templates:

- One with a sidebar,
- one full-width,
- and one for the blog.

This isn't always the case though, and they technically don't have to have any additional page templates if they don't want.

To see what a page template looks like, you may have to change it, save, and look at the live page to see what it actually looks like, but it's important to know that you do have options most of the time when it comes to how a page is laid out.

Now let's move on to our plugin we're going to use to build custom page layouts.

The plugin we're going to use this time is called Beaver Builder. I've used Beaver Builder in the past, and it seems to work well for building custom page layouts. (I also recommend Page Builder by SiteOrigin if you prefer that one.)

Once you've installed it, all you have to do is edit a page like normal, but this time click the Page Builder tab above the text editor.

You'll be taken to a live view of your page, where you can click and drag to add rows, with up to 6 columns, or add modules like a text editor or video, or you can add widgets directly onto your page.

Let's say we want 2 columns, so we click and drag that over to our page…

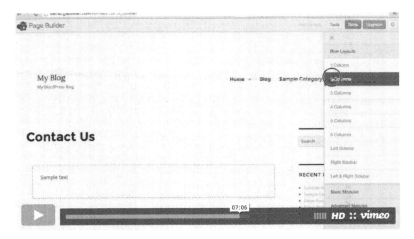

…and we want to add a photo on the left and a text editor on the right, where we'll add our shortcode for our contact form (you could also put a contact form widget in here, depending on the contact form plugin you're using).

Once you've added the photo and text editor with your contact form shortcode, you can click Done, and Publish Changes, and the changes should be live on your page now.

Here's the cool thing though:

Let's click Page Builder in our admin bar to go back and make more changes, and if we click one of our boxes…

…you can see that it lets us change the width, text color, background color, and borders of our section here:

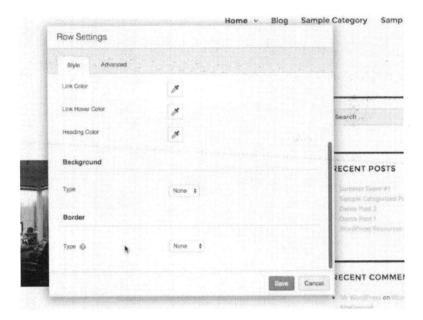

You can even click and drag to change the column widths if you want.

Contact Us

As you mess around with this plugin a bit, you'll see that you can create almost any look you want on your pages, which is something you would normally have to pay a web developer a pretty penny to do for you.

Now let me say, I ALWAYS recommend using your theme's options to customize your website whenever possible.

Using a plugin to customize your site seems convenient, but every plugin you run on your website slows your site down just a little bit more, and it's one more thing that can break.

Plugins are by no means bad to use, just make sure you always use your theme's options before resorting to using a plugin for customization.

Okay, so now we're able to customize our new website to get the look we want. After you've spent some time making your website look nice, we're going to talk about WordPress security and how to keep your site from getting hacked in the next section.

––––––––

For more advanced theme customization training, including how to create a child theme, please see the supplemental training videos that come free with this book.

You can access these videos by registering for your free membership at Gazellish.com/book.

16. OPTIMIZE YOUR SITE FOR SEO

No matter what you're planning on using your website for, chances are you're going to need some basic marketing tools so you can attract and build an audience.

For example, you'll want to make sure your site's following Search Engine Optimization (or SEO) best-practices so search engines can crawl and index your website without any hiccups.

You'll also want to make sure you have a way for people to join your email list directly from your website, because your email list will be one of the most valuable assets you have.

To get started, let's install one of the most popular WordPress plugins for SEO. It's called Yoast SEO, and it's free, so you can find it in the WordPress plugin repository.

Yoast SEO has a lot of features, including page analysis and recommendations, technical SEO, social integration, and much more.

We'll try to keep it simple for the sake of time, so we won't cover every feature in this section, but we'll cover a few of the main ones.

Let's go ahead and install Yoast SEO, and once it's activated, we can see that we now have a new section called SEO. We'll start by hovering over SEO, and clicking Social.

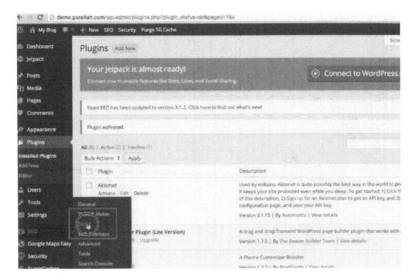

This is where you can "inform Google about your social profiles" – by entering the URLs of your social profiles.

One of the factors Google uses to rank websites is called social signals, so this will help "signal" Google of your social interaction and give the credit to your website.

Once you've done that, we're now going to click into Pages, and all the way to the right we can see there's now a column titled SEO. Each page has a circle that indicates its SEO score, ranging from red to green. As you can see below, right now none of them have a score because we haven't told our Yoast SEO plugin how to grade them yet.

Let's go in and edit one of our pages so we can see how to get Yoast to grade it.

Scroll down past the text editor, and towards the bottom you'll see the Yoast SEO section.

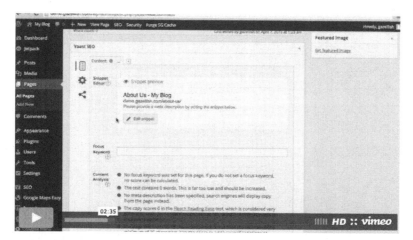

This is where we'll need to add a focus keyword, which tells Yoast what our page is about so it can give it a grade.

When we enter a focus keyword, we can now look at the content analysis just below that.

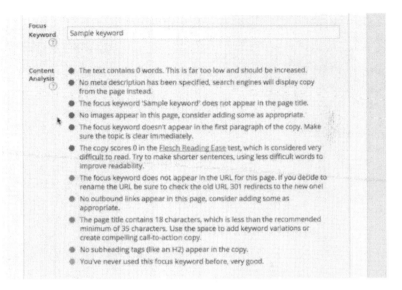

This is one feature that makes Yoast SEO so great – they give you a list of items to work on in order to make your page more search-engine-friendly.

Now click the Edit Snippet button just above the focus keyword in order to edit the SEO title, slug, and meta description. These are very important when it comes to SEO, so make sure you take time to got these right by including your keyword and making them unique for every page.

Let's look at one more thing here before we move on.

If you scroll up a bit and look on the left-hand side just under the Yoast SEO heading, you'll see 3 icons. Click the 3rd icon down – the social icon – and you'll see Facebook and Twitter options.

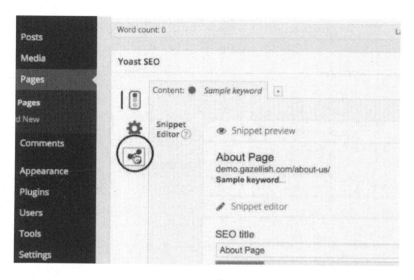

This is where you can manually change the title, description, and image displayed whenever someone posts a link to this page on Facebook or Twitter.

This may not seem like a very useful feature at first glance, but having a good title, description, and image displayed on social media will really help increase social interaction – which search engines love.

There are many other useful features in the Yoast SEO plugin, but we'll leave it at this for right now. As I mentioned before, we'll have more tutorials in the future that cover this plugin and other marketing and SEO plugins more in-depth.

For right now, one of the most important things you can do is make sure every page on your website has a unique title and description, and has a good rating (preferably a green rating) according to Yoast.

17. ADD SOCIAL SHARE BUTTONS

Alright, so now let's add one more quick plugin to our site. This one's called <u>Simple Social Icons</u> and, as you can probably guess, it's a social icons plugin.

This plugin will enable us to add icons to our site that link to our social media pages.

We'll install it and activate it...then go into our widgets, because that's where this plugin lives (I just happen to know that from experience).

Then scroll down a bit and you should see a widget called Simple Social Icons, and we'll drag that into one of our widget areas.

Once it's there, you'll see a dropdown with settings that let you change the icons' color and size, and you can also specify which icons you want to display by entering a URL into the field next to the appropriate label.

When you click save, and check out your site, you should see that you now have social icons in your widget area that link to our social media pages.

18. HOW TO TRANSFER A WORDPRESS WEBSITE

One thing you'll need to know at some point is how to move a WordPress site from one domain to another without losing any code or data.

If you've built your WordPress site on a test domain, if you've built it locally on your own computer, or if you simply want to move your site to a new domain name, you'll need to know how to transfer it without breaking anything.

You can transfer WordPress the "manual" way, but it's easy to break things that way.

Instead, we're first going to talk about how to go the easy route. By far the easiest and fastest way I've seen to move a WordPress site from one domain to another is to use a plugin called All-in-One WP Migration.

Here's the URL: wordpress.org/plugins/all-in-one-wp-migration/

BEFORE WE JUMP IN, THERE ARE A COUPLE OF STEPS TO TAKE IF YOU'RE REPLACING AN EXISTING WEBSITE WITH A WORDPRESS WEBSITE.

(If you're not replacing an existing website, skip to where it says "Here's how to migrate a WordPress website".)

If you're replacing an existing website with a new WordPress website, the first thing you should do is backup your existing website.

If your old website is a static HTML site, you can do this by connecting to your hosting account via FTP (using something like FileZilla), then transferring all of the files and folders of your old website into a single folder on your computer that you create. You can call this folder "old site", or something similar, with the date included in the name of the folder so you'll know what it is and when it was created.

You can also look for something that says "Backup" in your hosting account control panel. This is where you can create a full backup should you need to revert back for any reason. It never hurts to backup everything you can as often as you can, just in case something goes wrong.

When you're ready to move your new WordPress site to your actual domain, you'll need to start by moving your old website's files into a new folder so you'll have them for future reference. This will take your website down, so don't do this until you're 100% ready to make the switch.

To start, you can either use FTP or go back into your hosting account control panel, and click the link to go to the "file manager".

You'll want to create a new folder called "old-site" or whatever you want to call it. Again, it might help to include the date in the name of the folder, that way you remember when you created it if and when you come across it in the future.

Now move all your old website's files into this folder.

What we've essentially done is moved the entire old website into a folder that no one can see online, but that still remains on our hosting account's server should we ever need it in the future.

Once all the old website files are transferred into this "old-site" folder, you have a couple of options:

You can move your WordPress files and folders from your subdomain's folder (or "directory") into the same folder ("directory") your old website files and folders were in before you moved them.

If you do this, you'll have to make changes to your database and change URLs so your images and links won't be broken when you move the site.

OR

You can use a plugin to transfer your new WordPress site. And that's what we'll cover now.

Some developers may not agree, but I've found that using a plugin is much easier for beginners to move WordPress sites to a live domain without having to worry about breaking anything.

DON'T MAKE ANY CHANGES OR MOVE ANY WEBSITE FILES JUST YET.

You don't want to move your old website files into another folder without being able to replace them with your new WordPress site.

HERE'S HOW TO MIGRATE A WORDPRESS WEBSITE (THE EASY WAY)

Okay, so here's how to migrate a WordPress website using a plugin.

I've tried several plugins, and I've also done plenty of manual transfers, and All-in-One WP Migration is without a doubt the easiest.

Some people recommend manual transfers, which leave you in complete control over the transfer process. Transferring a WordPress website manually involves downloading or moving the WordPress files, exporting the database, then re-uploading everything to the new domain and changing information in the database. Then you have to make sure you use a separate plugin to change all the URLs from the old domain to the new one so all your links and images don't break.

Doing it that way is very time-consuming and you'll almost inevitably mess up somewhere along the way.

The other recommendation I hear a lot is to use a plugin called WP Clone. This plugin is actually the quickest and easiest plugin I've ever used to transfer a WordPress site, but the problem with it is, it rarely works. At least it did back when I was trying to use it on a regular basis.

WP Clone lets you create a backup, then it literally just gives you a URL to paste into their plugin on your new site (next to "restore from URL"), and in no time at all your site is transferred. It was amazing, the few times it actually worked.

I would say about 80% of the time I would get an error page whenever I tried to restore from a backup. It's a shame too, because whenever I needed to transfer a site, I would always go to WP Clone first because it's unbelievably simple and fast to use, only to have it give me some kind of error page when I tried to use it.

The people behind WP Clone may have worked those bugs out, but I gave up trying to use it. It might be worth giving it a look to see if it works for you.

All-in-One WP Migration, on the other hand, does the entire transfer process in a matter of minutes and very rarely does it ever give me a problem (and I've moved a ton of sites with it).

Every now and then the import process will get stuck and it's a little frustrating to have to start over, but it still pales in comparison to the frustration you'll face trying to do it manually.

To use All-in-One WP Migration to move a WordPress website, all you do is:

1. Install the All-in-One WP Migration plugin on your current site
2. Install WordPress and All-in-One WP Migration on the new domain
3. Use All-in-One WP Migration to export to a file on the old domain
4. Then use All-in-One WP Migration to import that file on the new site

And that's it!

The settings and import/export sections of All-in-One WP Migration are easy to find (you'll see them on the left-hand side of your WordPress dashboard once it's installed and activated), and the process is very intuitive.

However, as I said, every now and then it'll hang up on you and freeze in the middle of an import, but you can typically resolve that by redoing the process: re-exporting your site, then attempting to import the new export file.

Another way I've resolved this is by going directly into my website's files (either through FTP or cPanel) and manually adding the export file from All-in-One WP Migrate into the backups folder.

The backups folder is usually located just inside the wp-content folder, and should have the word "-backup" in the name of the folder.

You would just move your export file into this folder, then go back into the All-in-One WP Migration plugin dashboard in WordPress, go to the "Backups" section, refresh the page, then you should see the backup you just added in the list of backups. Click "Restore" and you should be good to go.

If you're having this issue, here's a great video on how to fix it:

youtube.com/watch?v=mRp7qTFYKgs

*That's not my video, so I apologize if it's no longer up.

IF YOU ABSOLUTELY MUST MIGRATE YOUR WORDPRESS WEBSITE MANUALLY, HERE'S HOW:

*FOR CLARITY, WE'RE GOING TO CALL THE SITE YOU'RE MOVING FROM "THE TEST SITE" AND WE'RE GOING TO CALL THE SITE YOU'RE MOVING TO "THE LIVE SITE".

STEP 1: CONNECT TO YOUR TEST WEBSITE'S HOST VIA FTP

If your test website is on your localhost, don't worry about this step.

Download software like FileZilla or Cyberduck, then use your FTP account credentials to connect to your host server. If you're not sure what your login credentials are for your FTP account, go to your hosting account control panel, then look for anything that says "FTP Accounts". You should be able to see your login info from there.

STEP 2: BACKUP YOUR TEST WEBSITE'S FILES AND FOLDERS

You basically need an exact replica of all of your test site's files and folders, so go ahead and create a new folder on your computer called "test-website" or anything else you like. Then you'll copy all of your WordPress files from your test site into this new folder on your computer.

STEP 3: EXPORT THE TEST SITE'S DATABASE.

To do this, go to your phpMyAdmin on your test site's host, select the database your test site is using, click export, then export the database. You should get a file that ends with ".sql".

STEP 4: ADD A NEW DATABASE FOR YOUR LIVE SITE

Now you need to add a new database to your live site's hosting account, so your WordPress site has a database to use when we move it over. You can do this by logging into your live site's hosting account control panel, then either go to your "MySQL® Databases" or phpMyAdmin for some local installs.

You'll have to create a new user or assign a user to this database. Make sure you know the login information for whichever user you add to this new database, because you'll need it in the next step.

STEP 5: EDIT YOUR WP-CONFIG.PHP FILE

Go to the folder on your local computer where you copied your website files to. In that folder, look for a file named "wp-config.php". Make another copy of this file and put it in a separate folder somewhere else on your computer, just in case anything breaks and you have to use this version of the file again.

Now open the wp-config.php file (the one in your "test-website" folder, not the copy you just made), and find the code that looks like this:

define('DB_NAME', 'your_db_name');

The "your_db_name" section should be set to the database name of your test site. This needs to be changed to the name of your live site's new database - the database you created in the previous step. Now change the database user. Look for this code:

define('DB_USER', 'your_db_user');

Change the "your_db_user" part from the username of your test site to the username of your live site's new database. Now change the database user password. The code will look like this:

define('DB_PASSWORD', 'your_db_pass');

Change the "your_db_pass" section to the password you created for your database user.

Now save and close the wp-config.php file.

STEP 6: IMPORT YOUR TEST SITE'S DATABASE

While you're still in phpMyAdmin, go ahead and select your live site's database, then click import, and import your test site's database file into your live site's database.

Once it's imported, click into the live site's database and go into "wp_options", then change any instance of your test site's URL to your live site's URL.

STEP 7: UPLOAD THE WORDPRESS FILES AND FOLDERS ON YOUR LIVE SITE.

Once you've added a database to your live site's host and you've updated your wp-config file, you'll need to go into your FTP client software, connect via FTP to your live site's host server and go to the directory (folder) of your live site. If the domain you're migrating to is the primary domain on the hosting account, you'll simply go to the root directory (which is usually just a folder called "public_html", "www", or something along those lines).

Now move all your test website's WordPress files into this folder where the live site will be.

STEP 8: CHANGE OUT ALL INSTANCES OF YOUR OLD URL IN YOUR SITE'S CONTENT.

You'll probably notice there are images or links that aren't working now. That's because they're still pointing to your test site. There are plugins that will fix this problem, one of which is called "Velvet Blues Update URLs".

This is the link at the time of this writing: wordpress.org/plugins/velvet-blues-update-urls/

This plugin finds all instances of your test site's URL and replaces them with your live site's URL. Just make sure you backup your site before running the plugin, that way you can revert back if anything breaks.

19. Good Plugins for New WordPress Websites

1. W3 Total Cache

Easy Web Performance Optimization (WPO) using caching: browser, page, object, database, minify and content delivery network support.

2. Akismet

Akismet checks your comments against the Akismet Web service to see if they look like spam or not.

3. Google XML Sitemaps

This plugin will generate a special XML sitemap which will help search engines to better index your blog.

4. Contact Form 7

Just another contact form plugin. Simple but flexible.

5. iThemes Security

Take the guesswork out of WordPress security. iThemes Security offers 30+ ways to lock down WordPress in an easy-to-use WordPress security plugin.

6. WP Smush

Reduce image file sizes, improve performance and boost your SEO using the free WPMU DEV WordPress Smush API.

7. ALL-IN-ONE WP MIGRATE

All-in-One WP Migration is the only tool that you will ever need to migrate a WordPress site.

8. YOAST SEO

Improve your WordPress SEO: Write better content and have a fully optimized WordPress site using Yoast SEO plugin.

9. DISABLE COMMENTS

Allows administrators to globally disable comments on their site. Comments can be disabled according to post type. Multisite friendly.

10. ALL IN ONE SCHEMA.ORG RICH SNIPPETS

Boost CTR. Improve SEO & Rankings. Supports most of the content type. Works perfectly with Google, Bing, Yahoo & Facebook.

11. BACKUP BUDDY

The #1 WordPress backup plugin.

12. SIMPLE SOCIAL ICONS

This plugin allows you to insert social icons in any widget area.

13. SUMOME

Free and easy way to double your email subscribers. Sharing tools to double your traffic from Facebook, Twitter, Pinterest & more.

14. PAGE BUILDER BY SITE ORIGIN

Build responsive page layouts using the widgets you know and love using this simple drag and drop page builder.

OR BEAVER BUILDER

The best drag and drop WordPress Page Builder. Easily build beautiful home pages, professional landing pages, and more with Beaver Builder.

20. Frequently Asked Questions About WordPress

I keep an updated list of frequently asked questions about WordPress at gazellish.com/wordpress-faq.

I highly suggest checking it out as you go along, and maybe even bookmarking it in your browser for when the moment comes and you need a quick answer!

21. Bonus: How to Start a Podcast Using WordPress

Podcasts are here to stay. And entrepreneurs everywhere are jumping on board.

In fact, a popular podcast hosting company called Libsyn reported that the number of podcasts hosted by them have more than doubled since 2008.

Okay, okay, I know. You've probably heard podcasting success stories, but for whatever reason maybe you haven't bought into the hype. Well, the data speaks for itself, and it says podcasting isn't just hype, and it isn't just a fad.

For example, did you know podcast listening grew 23% between 2015 and 2016?

How about the fact that monthly podcast listenership has increased 75% since 2013?

Short-term data is cool, but what about long-term numbers? Over the last 10 years, the number of people who have listened to a podcast has more than tripled.

As for regular listeners of podcasts, from 2008 to 2016, the percentage of US adults who listened to a podcast within the past month has more than doubled (from 9% to 21%).

That's right, 21% of US adults have listened to a podcast in the last month, indicating regular listenership. Think about that:

The number of people who listen to podcasts is about the same as the number of people on Twitter (21%). If you're an entrepreneur, that should at least make your ears perk up.

Now consider the fact that it's estimated by the year 2020, nearly all new cars will have internet connectivity. What do you think people will turn to for radio when they can connect to the Internet in their cars? You can't watch YouTube while you drive, and satellite radio still costs money. That leaves podcasts.

With all of that considered, you're talking about a bright future for podcasting.

Maybe you're just looking for a new way to build an audience for your business, or maybe you're looking to launch a new business venture altogether. Either way, podcasting is worth looking into at the very least.

And to top it all off, you can start your own podcast for really cheap (or even for free).

So if you decide to jump into podcasting - or just get your feet wet - here's how to start a podcast from scratch, for basically free.

MAKE A WEBSITE FOR YOUR PODCAST

Before creating your podcast and submitting it to iTunes, you'll need to have a place where your podcast episodes live and a feed that gets updated every time you publish a new episode. That's where your website comes in handy.

This is where WordPress is perfect. WordPress allows you to easily publish and organize your podcast episodes, and it automatically creates the proper RSS feed for your podcast.

If your website is not built in WordPress, I recommend learning how to use WordPress. You'll then need to either redesign your website in WordPress - which may not be ideal - or create a subdomain (yourpodcast.yourdomain.com) or subfolder (yourdomain.com/yourpodcast) and install WordPress there. Then you can build out a beautiful website just for your podcast, and you don't necessarily have to redesign your primary website to do it.

If you've made it this far in the book, chances are you already have a website up and ready to go. If so, carry on to the rest of this article.

FIND A MIC

Finding a podcasting microphone is really a matter of personal preference, but there are a few that stand out above the rest.

When it comes to all things podcasting, you'd be crazy not to listen to Pat Flynn. He has an insanely helpful article where he goes into his recommended microphones for podcasting.

The main 2 he recommends are:

- Heil PR-40
- Audio-Technica ATR2100USB

I would say go with the Audio-Technica starting out, then move to the Heil PR-40 down the road once you've gained some momentum.

I personally purchased the Audio-Technica and have been very pleased with its sound. It's clean, crisp, and doesn't have that "muffled" sound other mics have. You can't beat it for the price (I think it's around $79 on Amazon).

RECORD AND EDIT YOUR PODCAST EPISODES IN AUDACITY

If you do a little research, you'll probably find that Audacity is the industry standard for podcast beginners. It's easy to use, it's well-supported, and best of all, it's free.

To get started with Audacity, just head over to this site to download and install it. Then jump in and hit record. It'll probably take you a little time to get going and to understand the ins-and-outs of Audacity, but here's a tutorial to help you out.

HOST YOUR MEDIA FILES

Podcast episodes will weigh heavily on your regular web host if you try to upload them and host them directly on your site. Technically, you can do it, but it's not recommended.

I recommend hosting your podcast episodes at either Blubrry or Libsyn. Their plans start out pretty cheap for podcast hosting, and it's well worth it.

You can find all sorts of recommendations for podcast hosting on the web, but big names like Pat Flynn and Cliff Ravenscraft recommend Libsyn, so it's definitely worth taking a look at.

PUBLISH YOUR PODCASTS IN WORDPRESS

The first thing you'll want to do is download the Blubrry PowerPress plugin. Whether you're using Blubrry for your media hosting or not, this is still a good plugin to use to turn your WordPress site into a podcast platform.

Once it's installed and activated, head over to the PowerPress settings on the left-hand side of your dashboard, and fill out your podcast information.

This is where you'll add your iTunes category and artwork, among other things. These settings will be used in your RSS feed, which iTunes will use to populate your podcast.

The next thing you'll want to do is make sure you create a category specifically for your podcast episodes. This could just be called "Podcast", but you could get creative if you want.

For example, if you look at Pat Flynn's podcast feed, you can see his URL is smartpassiveincome.com/podcasts/feed/.

The "podcasts" in the URL is probably the name of his podcasts category, so that should help give you an idea as to why you need a separate category for your podcast. It just helps WordPress create a separate RSS feed for your podcast.

If you're going to have more than one podcast, or if your podcast posts will be labeled with more than one category, you'll want to enable "Category Podcasting". To do that, go to the PowerPress plugin settings, and scroll down to the Advanced Options section, then check the box next to where it says "Category Podcasting", then click save. Now on the left hand side of your dashboard under the PowerPress tab, you should see a new tab that says "Catcgory Podcasting". Click that, and you'll be taken to a page where you can tell the plugin which categories are your podcast categories.

When you have your settings updated and your podcast category created, all you have to do is:

CREATE A NEW POST

Select your podcast category (so it goes to the right RSS feed and signals iTunes that you have a new podcast episode)

Add content to the text editor, and write whatever intro, show notes, or other copy you want to add. You don't have to add another link to your audio file in the text editor, unless you just want to. Blubrry will automatically add it either before or after your post, depending on how you set it up in your Blubrry settings.

Then Scroll to the bottom of the page and you should see a "Podcast Episode" section. This is where you'll either enter the URL of your recording, or if you're using Blubrry for media hosting, you'll simply link your Blubrry account and select the file.

Hit publish and your podcast episode is now live. But we still have to do the most important part - submit our podcast to iTunes.

SUBMIT YOUR PODCAST TO ITUNES

Now we need to let iTunes know about our podcast so we can launch it and have it start populating in the iTunes Store.

To do that, we first need to make sure we have a few things in order. Blubrry says you'll need:

Artwork that is a square jpg or png formatted image at least 1400 x 1400 and at most 3000 x 3000 in size in RGB color space (1400 x 1400 jpg image recommended).

A unique podcast program title (check iTunes to make sure your program title is unique).

At least one iTunes category selected.

A valid email address in the iTunes email field (notifications from Apple will be sent to this address)

To have created at least one blog post with media (a podcast episode) in either mp3, m4a, mp4, m4v, PDF, or EPUB format.

When you're ready to submit your podcast to iTunes:

Go to podcastsconnect.apple.com.

Click the "+" button at the top left.

Enter the RSS feed URL of your podcast and click "Validate". Typically, your feed will look like…

http://www.yourdomain.com/podcast/feed

…but it could be different if you're using the category podcasting feature). Usually with WordPress, you can just slap "/feed" at the end of the URL for a category, and you'll get the feed for that category.

You should see all of the information and artwork for your podcast. If everything looks good, click "Submit".

After you've submitted your podcast, be patient. It could take anywhere from a few hours to a matter of days. Apple should send you an email with your podcast's URL once it's approved.

You'll need to copy this URL (your actual podcast URL) and paste it into your Blubrry PowerPress plugin settings under the iTunes section in the iTunes subscribe URL section.

Once your podcast has been approved, you're ready to start podcasting and building your audience!

When you're ready to get started creating your podcast, take the first step by learning how to quickly build a beautiful WordPress site for your podcast for free.

Now What?

Congratulations! You've made it to the end of the book, which means you should have a beautiful, functional website live on the web.

People pay thousands of dollars to have that done for them, and you just did it for yourself. Pat yourself on the back!

Here are a few things you can (and should) do now:

Keep your site updated

One of the biggest problems I see with WordPress sites is people building their website then rarely updating it again. This leaves your website and your hosting account vulnerable to attacks, and it can also cause issues with your site if you let it go too long.

WordPress does a good job of letting you know when there's an update for a theme, plugin, or WordPress itself, so don't ignore them! Those updates are important.

Ask Questions

By purchasing this book, you've been given access to a community of other WordPress users at Gazellish.com.

When you have questions, use the forums and the email support that come as a part of your membership.

You'll get your questions answered and you'll get support most other beginners have to pay for or dig for hours online to find.

ONE LAST THING

If you enjoyed this book or found it useful in any way, I'd really appreciate it if you would post a short review on Amazon.

I read all the reviews personally, and they help guide me on what topics to cover in future editions of the book, as well as which videos to add to the membership part of Gazellish.com (which you have access to with this book).

Thanks for your support!